KNOW YOUR SPECTRUM!

of related interest

I am Special
A Workbook to Help Children, Teens and Adults with Autism Spectrum Disorders to Understand Their Diagnosis, Gain Confidence and Thrive
Peter Vermeulen
ISBN 978 1 84905 266 5
eISBN 978 0 85700 545 8

My Autism Book
A Child's Guide to their Autism Spectrum Diagnosis
Glòria Durà-Vilà and Tamar Levi
ISBN 978 1 84905 438 6
eISBN 978 0 85700 868 8

The Asperger Teen's Toolkit
Francis Musgrave
ISBN 978 1 78592 161 2
eISBN 978 1 78450 438 0

Using Poetry to Promote Talking and Healing
Pooky Knightsmith
Foreword by Catherine Roche and Dr Fiona Pienaar
ISBN 978 1 78592 053 0
eISBN 978 1 78450 323 9

Developing Identity, Strengths, and Self-Perception for Young Adults with Autism Spectrum Disorder
The BASICS College Curriculum
Michelle Rigler, Amy Rutherford and Emily Quinn
ISBN 978 1 84905 797 4
eISBN 978 1 78450 095 5
Part of The BASICS College Curriculum *series*

The Social and Life Skills MeNu
A Skill Building Workbook for Adolescents with Autism Spectrum Disorders
Karra M. Barber
ISBN 978 1 84905 861 2
eISBN 978 0 85700 433 8

The ASD Workbook
Understanding Your Autism Spectrum Disorder
Penny Kershaw
ISBN 978 1 84905 195 8
eISBN 978 0 85700 427 7

KNOW YOUR SPECTRUM!

AN AUTISM CREATIVE WRITING WORKBOOK FOR TEENS

FINN MONAHAN

Jessica Kingsley *Publishers*
London and Philadelphia

First published in 2019
by Jessica Kingsley Publishers
73 Collier Street
London N1 9BE, UK
and
400 Market Street, Suite 400
Philadelphia, PA 19106, USA

www.jkp.com

Library of Congress Cataloging in Publication Data
A CIP catalog record for this book is available from the Library of Congress

British Library Cataloguing in Publication Data
A CIP catalogue record for this book is available from the British Library

ISBN 978 1 78592 435 4

Printed and bound in the United States

For my parents

For Darren,
Jamie and Daniel

Contents

Preface

Being autistic means that we experience the world around us differently to other people. Autism is usually described as a spectrum that is external to us and we are thought to be somewhere on the autistic spectrum. While this perspective is useful, I think it is also important to understand autism from the internal experiences of the individual. This book is based on the idea that autism is a spectrum that lies within us. We each have our own particular autistic behaviours, with the commonly associated strengths and challenges which are unique to each of us. By learning to identify our personal version of autism we can understand who we are. This is important as autism can mean that we sometimes feel different and we might try to change ourselves to be like other people. However, if we are comparing ourselves to someone who is not considered to be autistic, then we will be constantly trying to fit inside a mould that is not made for us. Trying to adapt to other people's way of doing things is exhausting for us and can lead to lots of problems that we can perhaps avoid by simply finding out what works for us and what doesn't, and how other people can help us to reduce any barriers in society that we may have to deal with.

Our starting point in this book is my own perspective on how my autism makes me feel and behave. The reader is then encouraged to think about how their own autism affects their feelings and behaviour. This will allow us to understand ourselves and establish a sense of identity that is true for us and find out what things feel good for us and how we can live in a way that makes us happy. In turn, this self-awareness will allow us to recognise our patterns of behaviour and we can start to develop strategies specific to our needs that will help us to cope with any difficulties we are experiencing.

Through creating a solid foundation of self-knowledge based on our personal spectrum of autism we will have a greater chance of fulfilling our potential. Acknowledging our autism will let us be ourselves and do everything we want to in a way that makes life easier for us. Whether we are autistic or not, each person is born with their own personality and natural way of doing things. We can only be who we are and let our spectrum of autism shine through.

About This Book

I wrote this book to help autistic teenagers to find out about themselves and work out their individual spectrum of autism. It is written from the perspective of an autistic person and the contents are mostly inspired by my experiences of growing up with undiagnosed autism.

The book can be completed by teenagers on their own or with help from family or teachers. It consists of a series of worksheets and writing activities for teenagers which they can continue to use even when this book is finished. I provide completed versions of all the activities to give a comprehensive overview of my autism that the teenagers can refer to. This design is intended to support the teenagers' thought processes and creativity while allowing them to compare and contrast themselves against another autistic person to establish their unique autism spectrum. Through completing the activities the teenagers will be able to establish what their strengths are and any areas that they may need support with. The teenagers can then begin to develop strategies to help them cope with any difficulties they are experiencing.

The book provides an in-depth look at the various issues that autistic individuals may have to deal with, using an approach with similarities to cognitive behavioural therapy (CBT) programmes. It offers the teenagers an opportunity to record and reflect on what is happening in their lives. They are encouraged to think through their emotions in terms of how they present in both their body and mind, to help them develop an understanding of their feelings. Through improving awareness of their emotions the teenagers can learn to spot when they are becoming overwhelmed so they can develop self-care strategies. In learning to observe their behaviours the teenagers may gradually develop the skills to monitor their reactions to reduce the impact of factors such as shutdowns or meltdowns.

Writing their experiences down will allow the teenagers to release any internal tension over situations which otherwise may build up over time if they are not able to recognise or verbalise their feelings. This opportunity to express their emotions is further extended by the addition of a creative element, with a range of writing styles demonstrated in my example worksheets including poems, thoughts, mini-stories and narratives. It is anticipated that the teenagers can continue to explore their creative writing beyond this book and hoped that they can find an additional means of expressing themselves. The teenagers may start to use creative writing as an emotional support strategy in the longer term, leading to a greater ability to manage their emotions and further extend their self-knowledge and self-awareness. As this form of writing requires a different kind of thought process and style of language, it allows for everything that has been learnt to be recapped within an alternative framework, potentially leading to a deeper understanding of the issues covered. In addition this creative element may help to develop the teenagers' creative writing skills and lead to the discovery of hidden talents.

The book is designed to bring all the different parts of autism together into one coherent structure so that the interaction between autism and how it presents in the teenagers' daily life can be observed. This will allow for issues that may never have been discussed to be addressed and possibly prevent a lot of misunderstandings and problems from developing. The activities also provide the opportunity for the teenagers to begin to develop self-advocacy skills by outlining what they would like other people to know about the various topics covered. The book can be used as a support tool on a continuous basis, with the potential for the teenagers to create a personal profile separate to the book describing their autism spectrum. By following the structure adopted by the book, the teenagers, parents and teachers will benefit from the deeper insights it will bring, while it should also allow the teenagers confidence to grow in themselves as autistic people.

I hope that through this creative and interactive learning process the teenagers will gain a sense of empowerment in learning about who they are while actively taking control in recognising, celebrating and managing their spectrum of autism.

Aims of the Book for Teenagers

- Learn about our unique spectrum of autism.

- Become more aware of our behaviour, reactions and how autism impacts on different situations.

- Begin to identify and express our emotions.

- Recognise the connections between cause and effect in our daily life.

- Establish what we need help with and strategies to deal with issues.

- Create a profile of our strengths to build on.

- Develop our skills of self-reflection.

- Increase our self-advocacy skills by outlining what we would like other people to know.

- Be able to plan and prepare for future events so we can be in control of who we are.

- Encourage communication with families and/or teachers.

- Enable parents, families and teachers to gain a greater understanding of our autism.

- Build friendships with peers when attending the seven-week course (see How to Use The Book as a Course).

- Explore our creative writing skills.

How to Use This Book

Teenagers, parents and families

This book can be used by teenagers on their own to work through issues and learn about themselves and they can choose to share the results with family and friends if they feel able to.

Parents can also support their teenager's progress, which will give them a greater appreciation of what autism means for their child. This will allow for the necessary support to be given in a way that will be specific to the teenager's personal spectrum of autistic behaviours and their strengths and challenges. The contents can be used to develop discussions between families, including siblings, which may help to strengthen bonds and understanding of what is happening underneath the surface of those family members who are on the autism spectrum.

The information provided within each chapter builds upon the previous topic to allow for the reader's understanding of autism to develop across the book. To get the most out of the book it is advised that the chapters are completed in the order given. However, the activity sections within each chapter can be completed in any order. There may be individual sections of each chapter that the teenager has not yet experienced and they can be left until a later stage if needed.

As writing can be a gradual process, it might be helpful for the teenagers to use a rough notebook for their first draft before filling in the actual activity book.

Activities

Within the activity sheets provided, Finn's completed examples include a range of thoughts and points which aim to outline issues relevant to the teenagers. These are intended to offer a template for the teenagers to compare and contrast themselves against in order to identify their own autism spectrum. The teenager is further supported by the inclusion of additional writing prompts for each activity section offering alternative perspectives or asking relevant questions. The teenagers can complete the worksheet within the book; any creative writing will require an additional writing pad.

Each activity section contains a selection of related poems, thoughts, mini-stories or narratives written by Finn. A variety of styles are included to ensure the teenagers feel comfortable in whichever suits them best and to inspire their creativity. The book is structured to ensure that a wide range of ability levels are able to successfully write in a creative way. To achieve this, poems vary from one-line thoughts or very simple statements to more expressive styles of writing combined with longer single-piece narratives. Teenagers can use lines from Finn's completed activities as writing prompts and use the questions provided to guide them through each topic. If needed, a line from one poem can be put together with another line from another to build them up into one poem to help those teenagers who find it difficult to get started or to write poems. Alternatively the teenagers can use their own creativity to write independently and just follow the overall structure of the chapter's activities.

When the book is completed the main activities can all be repeated again at any stage, using different experiences to extend the teenager's understanding of what is happening in their lives.

As the book is based on the author's experiences and interpretation of autism, if there is an activity topic that the teenager does not relate to, then they can adjust the titles to suit the perspective that they would like to write about.

The book is written from the perspective of the author, Finn. The terms 'I, me, us, we, our' are used to refer to someone with autism. In the writing prompts for each chapter the words 'you' and 'your' are used to refer to the teenagers; 'they' and 'other people' are used to refer to people who are not autistic. In Finn's creative writing sections, the terms 'you', 'your', 'they' and 'other people' are referring to non-autistic people.

Chapter Structure

The format in all the chapters is repeated throughout the book for ease of use as follows:

Introduction

Each chapter opens with an explanation of the topic theme, how it relates to autism and what this can mean for an autistic person.

Activities (1–4 per chapter)

The activities within each chapter are divided into one to four individual topics to be covered, with a series of activity sheets and writing prompts provided related to each area.

Each activity section within a chapter includes:

- **Finn's worksheet:** This outlines the author's own spectrum of autism for each topic.

- **Finn's creative writing:** Finn's activity sheet is used as the basis for completing her creative writing element.

- **Writing prompts:** These consist of questions for the teenagers to support them in completing each writing activity.

- **Teenagers' worksheet:** This is to be filled in by the teenagers to help them work out their spectrum of autistic behaviours for each theme covered.

What's my spectrum?

This section allows for an overview of the teenagers' personal spectrum of autism in relation to each chapter's theme. The teenagers can learn to identify their positive attributes and develop their awareness of any challenges in terms of how they can deal with them or what they may need help with. It concludes with the teenagers beginning to develop self-advocacy skills through outlining what they would like other people to know. This will enable them to be better understood and get the specific support they need.

Activities include:

- **Finn's worksheet:** Finn records her personal spectrum of autistic characteristics for the chapter topics.

- **Teenagers' worksheet:** Teenagers record their own spectrum of autistic characteristics for each chapter theme.

- **Finn's creative writing**: This outlines the topics covered in each worksheet.

- **Teenagers' creative writing activity sheet:** This provides space for the teenagers to write creatively about their spectrum of each chapter topic.

- **My profile chart:** Each chapter finishes with a table that allows the teenagers to summarise the main points they have learnt about themselves for each topic covered.

Note: In Chapter 7, *Know Your Spectrum of Self-Regulation, Routines and Interests*, there is an additional activity allowing the teenagers to list their interests and routines with the related advantages and disadvantages outlined too. Within the activity section the teenager has the opportunity to outline three different interests and then they can pick one, or all three if they wish, to write about creatively.

How to Use the Book as a Course

Teachers, counsellors and adults working with autistic teenagers

Teachers and adults working with autistic teenagers can use the book as the basis of an autism self-awareness course to be run over a seven-week period in a school setting or as an independent autistic teenager support group.

If the group is run by an autistic adult they could complete the worksheets to give an additional example for the teenagers to follow.

The ideal size of group would be approximately six to eight teenagers to allow for relationships to develop and create a sense of intimacy and trust in sharing personal stories.

The length of time to complete a full chapter can be decided individually but it would be expected that the optimum time for a class would be two hours. Or the chapters could be split and run over two separate hour-long sessions.

It is hoped that there would be potential for the writing groups to continue on a long-term basis, helping the teenagers to build a network of friendships that could prove vital as they continue through this potentially difficult stage in their life.

The book can also be used on a read-only basis by anyone interested in autism and used as a group discussion tool to think about the various topics highlighted.

Course timings

Introductory explanation (10–15 minutes)

The introductory explanation can be used to open the weekly discussion, encouraging the teenagers to open up about what this particular area of autism means for them.

Activities (1–4 in each chapter; 20–30 minutes per section)

The teacher can lead students through Finn's examples to generate discussions and ideas. Support can then be given to help the teenagers think of situations to write about, allowing them to identify their positive attributes and what they may need help with. Important events that have happened in the teenagers' lives can be considered, including the effect on their emotions and the connections between cause and effect. Teachers can help the teenagers to develop suitable strategies to deal with the issues highlighted.

What's my spectrum of...? (15 minutes)

At the end of the session the group leader can help the teenagers to bring together the key points identified so that they can describe their spectrum of autistic behaviours in terms of their strengths and challenges for each chapter topic. This can be followed by a recap of what has been learnt to support the teenagers when completing their profile chart.

Optional

An extra week could be added onto the course to allow for the teenagers to finish off any activities and share their completed *Know Your Spectrum!* book with the group if they wish.

Author's Introduction

My name is Finn, and if you're reading this book then you must be like me and have a diagnosis of autism. Or you might know someone with autism and are trying to get a better understanding of them. Autism has lots of different aspects to it which are often not well understood. This book aims to help us find out more about all the various things that make up what is called the spectrum of autism while allowing us to identify our own personal spectrum of autism within. By doing this we will learn to recognise our strengths and at the same time we will find out how to manage the areas we find tricky to deal with.

How we experience our autism in daily life is also influenced by other people's reactions to our autism. Autism can often be misjudged and misunderstood and sometimes that can be the most difficult part of being autistic. To overcome these kinds of issues we can share our creative writing from this book to help others appreciate what is going on inside us and maybe prevent communication breakdowns from developing.

The process of writing about our personal experiences will allow us to express our thoughts and feelings. This is important as we can find it hard to work out our emotions, but writing about what has happened and how we feel may prevent us from becoming overwhelmed. It will also gradually help us to understand who we are. Autism can mean that we aren't able to 'see' ourselves in a way that we can relate to and everything is very confusing to work out. Writing makes things that are abstract more tangible, rather than just separate thoughts floating around in our minds that might not make much sense. There are all different sorts of writing included within the book and sometimes it can be intimidating to try to write a poem or put our intimate thoughts onto paper. That's normal to feel that way and don't worry if you feel you can't write poems or don't know what to say sometimes. This is your book and there is no right way of writing, only your way. I think the best way to write is to focus on expressing yourself and forget about whether it's good enough or not. It is!! Just write, get the words down, and let them lead you through all the different situations and experiences that come up during the process and you will gradually find out what you need to learn. It might be that you have not really had to deal with some topics covered in the book, and if that is the case you can leave that section to another time or adjust the titles to make it fit with something that you have experienced. You can choose to work through the book independently or with help from your families, teachers or group leaders – whatever you feel most comfortable with and ready for.

This book is written from my experiences, based on how autism presents in me both now and as a teenager with various situations outlined that describe my daily life. I might seem very similar to you or the complete opposite. There are many different ways of being autistic; no two people are the same. How we experience autism depends on who we are as individuals and how our bodies and minds work. We might have lots of sensory things going on but not too many processing differences, or it may be the other way round. How our autism presents can change from day to day and it is not static. Like most people, we will have good days when we are able to cope and bad days when everything is much harder to deal with.

Whatever our experiences, both our personalities and our spectrum of autism are unique to us. By thinking about the different aspects of autism outlined within this book, you will have a chance to get to know your autism spectrum. I hope you enjoy the journey.

Know Your Spectrum

To know our spectrum
Helps us to see
Who we are
What we can be.

It might take some thinking
With some writing too
A few mini-stories
A poem or two.

There's a lot of work to do
To get to the end.
But it might be worth it
To get a different view.

Our autism can bring
Many wonderful things.
It also can mean
A different way of being.

With a word that's shared
A story that's told
They may bring us together,
Help avoid those divides.

So let's figure it out
Then we'll know what to do
To help us find
Our place in this world.

Chapter 1

Know Your Spectrum of Executive Functioning

Introduction

Executive functioning covers a whole range of areas in the brain which help us to do things. It influences our ability to make decisions, be organised and plan our activities.

Organisation and prioritisation

We can have really good organisational skills and excel in this area so everything we have is in perfect order with highly efficient systems in place, or we may be totally disorganised. Our ability to be organised might change, and in some ways we can be super-organised and other areas work without any structure at all. Estimating and managing time to get things completed for deadlines can also be a challenge (Attwood 2008).

We might find it hard to prioritise and decide which task is most important and therefore needs to be completed first and what can wait until later. This could result in us not getting anything done at all, as we can't make up our minds which task to do first. It can be difficult for us to know how to start working on a task and to actually get up and take action as we might get stuck in a state of inertia which means we can't get anything done.

Rigid/focused thinking and setting goals

Once we do start a task it can be even more difficult to stop as we may struggle to monitor our actions. We tend to just keep going without changing our focus or adjusting our behaviour to adapt to what is happening inside our bodies or around us. If we are hungry we might not stop and get something to eat. Instead we keep going and ignore our body's needs as we are completely focused on getting the task finished.

We have an intense desire to work from start to finish without detours of any kind. Anything that interrupts this process might irritate us as it can be frustrating and hard to stop and change our focus or cope with several demands at once. Doing more than one task at a time requires us to continually shift our focus from one task to another which is not our natural way of working.

We need to actively make our minds change focus from one thought or activity to another, which takes a lot of mental effort, and we don't really want to stop anyway. We tend to hyper-focus, which can be very useful in allowing us to develop an expertise in our particular interests. But it can also mean that sometimes our minds get stuck and we can end up doing too much, or maybe even becoming obsessed. Or we might be easily distracted, and if we are interrupted we will lose track of what we were thinking or doing.

Our rigid thinking style can lead to seeing things in a very black and white way. For example, we might have an opinion on an event and whatever we have decided might become absolutely the only version, and we could have trouble taking into account all the other possible explanations. Our thoughts could then get stuck on some specific points that we might have a tendency to keep repeating over and over in our minds, making us get more and more annoyed or depressed about it.

It might not occur to us that there is a different way to do something other than how we have got used to doing it. We may not be able to see all the options that other people do and so what makes sense for us may seem unusual to others. This can cause problems as people think we are being rigid on purpose or being uncooperative when we stick to our way of doing something or find it hard to cope with changes. We prefer to stick to one method and we can become so attached to it that it is hard to alter our behaviour. We tend to keep using the same methods over and over again even when they are not working (Attwood 2008).

We can also have a great deal of focus and attention to detail that most people don't have. Because we see so much detail we can sometimes miss the broader picture of events, so we will have a different perspective to other people. This means we think of things that no one else would, which is a very useful skill to have. Our higher level of focus means we can get a lot done within our selected area of interest and gives us an advantage in helping us to achieve our goals.

Memory

Our strong long-term memory means we can remember lots of facts and information from a long time ago. But our short-term memory might not be so good. We might forget or mix up verbal messages and instructions that we have just heard or forget what we were talking about.

Our short-term memory also affects our ability to monitor what we are doing. It allows us to work out how we are doing at tasks and how well our strategies are working. Being able to monitor our behaviour allows us to identify when we need to change our methods. Our minds have difficulty being flexible and adjusting our behaviours or strategies when necessary as we can't see all the options when completing tasks (Attwood 2008).

Impulsivity

When we make a mistake we don't always learn from it so that we know what to do the next time. Our minds go in straight lines as if we are on a train track with no gears to change direction or adjust our intensity and speed (Attwood 2008). Knowing when we need to stop and think about what we are doing or saying can be hard for us to do. This can lead us to have impulsive behaviour and then we might say or do things without registering the consequences (Attwood 2008). It can also appear that we are being rude or insensitive by saying what we think. When we are stressed, overwhelmed or confused we might become more impulsive and unable to monitor our actions, which can lead to arguments or get us into trouble (Attwood 2008).

We need to figure out what things we are good at doing and identify what we find difficult.

Then we can learn to manage our executive functioning skills and make the most of our strengths and build on those areas we find harder to cope with. We can make sure that we make the most of our intensely focused minds to help us to achieve all our goals.

This section outlines Finn's style of organisation and prioritisation. It can be used as a template to identify your own spectrum of organisation and prioritisation.

Finn's spectrum of organisation and prioritisation

Activity: What does Finn have problems organising or prioritising?

- Paperwork, forms and folders.
- Bags, drawers and cupboards.
- Keeping track of the correct dates to attend events.
- Understanding and estimating time to meeting deadlines.
- Getting out in the mornings at the time planned.
- Cooking several things at one time and following recipes if necessary.

Activity: What is Finn good at organising or prioritising?

- Structuring essays.
- Travel plans – what places to visit, what to do and in what order.
- Creating music playlists.
- Wall displays of her photo collection of 1950s movie stars.

Strategies: To help Finn stay organised and prioritise she can:

- make clear plans in a daily, weekly and monthly timetable
- set realistic deadlines for specific tasks that she can meet
- create colour-coded spidergrams to plan out tasks
- write down what is important, what can wait and what can be forgotten.

Finn's spectrum of organisation and prioritisation

Read Finn's creative writing. What organisation and prioritisation challenges does Finn face?

Organisational challenges

My bag

It's very, very sticky
It's really rather icky
I am in fact so lucky
Despite it being quite mucky
It hasn't come alive
Attracting bees from their hive.
To sort it I can't bear
And now I just don't care.
I leave it far too long
It looks terribly wrong.
Oh, it's such a pain
What do I have to gain?
Well maybe a little cleaning time
Would mean half the grime
Then surely I will find
A little peace of mind.

Organisational strengths

Where to go?
What to do?
Travel plans
Far over sea.
Leave it to me
To get ordered and sorted.
No trouble at all!

Finn's strategies to stay organised and prioritise her tasks

To do

Coursework...must be done on time!

Wait a minute

Organising paperwork... in a pile in the corner.

Forget it!!

Bag...it will do as it is.

ACTIVITY A. MY WRITING PROMPTS

My spectrum of organisation and prioritisation

Use the following vocabulary prompts and questions to complete your worksheet and then write your own poems, thoughts, mini-stories or narrative for each topic below.

Word prompts

Disorganisation: Muddled, chaos, disorder, scrambled, disarray, junk, mess, piles, stack, stress, clutter, confusion, jumble, demotivated, anxiety.

Organisation and prioritisation: Sorted, cataloguing, categories, micro-manage, focused, alphabetical, numerical, sequence, arranged, classification, systematic, logical, empowering, motivated, ordered, priority, control.

Activity: What do I have problems organising and prioritising?

What do you have the most difficulty keeping in order? Why is this hard? Is it because you have too much stuff, there are too many parts to know what to do?

What problems does disorganisation cause at home or in school? Can you work out what tasks are important and what to leave so you can get started?

Activity: What am I good at organising and prioritising?

Are you good at organising one big task or lots of small, detailed tasks? Are you good at developing systems, e.g. sorting books and CDs into alphabetical order?

Strategies: To help me stay organised and prioritise I can:

Would it help to identify what jobs you need help with and who can support you? Could charts or photos on files act as visual supports? Do you find tick lists helpful? Would a clock timer help you to start and finish tasks?

My spectrum of organisation and prioritisation

Record your thoughts and experiences here.

Activity: What do I have problems organising and prioritising?

....

....

....

....

Activity: What am I good at organising and prioritising?

....

....

....

....

Strategies: To help me stay organised and prioritise I can:

....

....

....

....

This section outlines Finn's memory spectrum. It will help you identify your own memory profile.

Finn's spectrum of memory

Short-term memory	Long-term memory
Finn is not good at remembering... • *messages* • *instructions* • *practical tasks* • *names*	*Finn is good at remembering...* • *topics studied* • *film scenes* • *conversations* • *song lyrics.*

Finn's problems with short–term memory might mean:

• *she gets stressed if she can't remember messages*

• *she feels stupid and not very useful if she keeps getting things mixed up*

• *she becomes frustrated because she seems to get things wrong even when she tries hard to remember.*

Finn's good long–term memory might mean:

• *revision topics stick in her head, with no problem to recollect*

• *negative events, from long ago in the past, might never leave her mind.*

Strategies: To help Finn remember stuff she can:

• *make an image in her mind which connects to the topic*

• *relate things to a song/picture/poem*

• *ask for information to be repeated and maybe written down too.*

Finn's spectrum of memory

Read Finn's creative writing. What kind of things does Finn have trouble remembering and what is she good at never forgetting?

Short-term memory

The correct milk bottle
Green, red or blue
Three times I told you!!!
The bacon for tea
Smoked or unsmoked...
Ten times I told you!!!!
Because my memory is stuck
On the first and maybe the third
Word that I just heard
Still ringing loud in my ear
The rest, it would appear,
I didn't actually hear.
And I won't even try
With numbers that make me cry.
But maybe a note
That I can keep in my coat
Will help me recall
All the words I was told.
Then I won't walk into a wall
As I mutter to myself

What was I supposed to do??

Long-term memory

Conversations I had
From 5, 10, even 20 years ago.
I never seem to forget words
When they are part of a story.
They have a meaning and an image
That stays perfectly clear.
A film in my mind
I can rewind
To watch at any time.

What Finn's forgetful short–term memory means

My slightly wobbly short-term memory lets me down each day. Words spoken two minutes ago, but I can hardly remember the beginning of the sentence. Now I seem to have forgotten the last bit too.

It makes me feel so very useless to not be able to recall these simple things. I am trying my hardest but I can't seem to get it right.

Don't even ask if I can take this message... No, I definitely cannot!!!

What Finn's good long—term memory means

That argument, from long ago, never shifted out of my brain. Fact and detail stay perfectly clear. If you are a police detective, I am the person you want on your team!

Finn's strategies to remember stuff

Colour and charts
Words and images too.
Simple songs
Musical tunes.
Repeat and review
Puts everything I need to know
Safely stored in my extraordinarily good
Long-term memory.

ACTIVITY C. YOUR WRITING PROMPTS

My spectrum of memory

Use the following vocabulary prompts and questions to complete your worksheet and then write your own poems, thoughts, mini-stories or narrative for each topic below.

Word prompts

Memory: Recall, recollect, evaporate, disappear, frustrating, vanish, dissolve, exasperating, confusion, exceptional, accurate, photographic, detailed, powerful, extraordinary, factual, realistic, exact, clear, reliable, consistent.

How does my memory work?

What do you find difficult to remember? This might include long messages with complicated instructions.

What do you find easy to remember? Are you good at remembering facts?

My problems with short–term memory might mean:

Do you sometimes get annoyed because you can't remember what you were supposed to do? Are instructions hard to follow? When do you find this is most challenging?

My good long–term memory might mean:

Can you remember lots of things which have made you feel bad? Do you remember facts very accurately? Are you good at remembering lines from songs and movies?

Strategies: To help me remember stuff I can:

How can you use your strengths to help you remember what is important? Can you use visual clues or photographs?

Are digital calendars and reminders useful for you to stay organised?

ACTIVITY D. MY WORKSHEET

My spectrum of memory

Record your thoughts and experiences here.

Short-term memory	Long-term memory
I am not good at remembering…	I am good at remembering…
•	•
•	•
•	•

My problems with short–term memory might mean:

_____

_____

_____

My good long–term memory might mean:

_____

_____

_____

Strategies: To help me remember stuff I can:

_____

_____

_____

This section outlines Finn's spectrum of rigid/focused thinking and setting goals. You can use this as a template to work out your own spectrum of rigid/focused thinking and setting goals.

Finn's spectrum of rigid/focused thinking and setting goals

Event: When does this happen to Finn?

Finn's rigid thoughts get stuck on:	*Finn is highly focused when:*
• *problems she doesn't know how to solve*	• *there are targets to achieve, deadlines to meet*
• *repeating thoughts*	• *taking part in activities/sports*
• *cleaning and washing*	• *spotting details that no one else can see*
• *sitting in a certain chair*	• *developing an in-depth knowledge of her interests*
• *songs/words/hobbies*	• *doing courses*
• *routines and rituals*	• *working in her job*
• *eating certain foods*	• *daydreaming.*
• *arguments.*	

Meaning: What does this mean for Finn?

- *Negative thoughts lead to a depressed mind which further darkens with this rigid stuck mind.*

- *She can't change focus from one activity to another or stop when she needs to.*

- *Single-minded focus that does not adjust easily has both potential and difficulties.*

- *Targets create a channel for her potential to expand. She sees only what she is focused on. The goal!*

Strategies: To help Finn change her thoughts she can:

- move her body to shift her mindset

- write down what is annoying her, then rip it up and throw it away to get rid of any negative thoughts or anger

- write a list of things that she is really enthusiastic about and she wants to start doing immediately and then start doing them to take her attention away from things she has got stuck on.

Goals: To help Finn achieve her goals she can:

- take her mistakes as lessons and use everything she learns to do better next time

- ignore failures and keep resetting her targets when necessary

- focus on what she wants and pay no attention to what other people think she can or cannot do. She is the only person who knows what she is capable of

- adopt a positive mental attitude – thinking good thoughts and believing that she can achieve anything she wants

- visualise what she wants.

Finn's spectrum of rigid/focused thinking and setting goals

Read Finn's creative writing. How does Finn's thinking style influence her daily life?

Finn's rigid and focused thoughts

Problems
Problems
Everywhere
Focused thoughts become a blur.
Targets
Targets
Straight ahead
Focused thoughts
Make me succeed!

Finn's thought-changing strategies

Write
It
Out.
Rip
It
Up.
Let
It
Go.
Start
Again!

Meaning for Finn

Thoughts on repeat
Negativity breeds
Stuck on a loop
Motivation goes.

Positive focus
Flows and grows
End-point target
Accomplished goal!

Finn's goal achievement

Positive Mental Attitude

Will take me anywhere I want to go.
The more I think I can do it
The more chance I have of succeeding
Regardless of things that seem
too much for me to overcome.

Visualisation in my imagination
Of what I want in the greatest detail
Write it out with every aspect of
my target goal considered
Focus, dream, work.
Focus, dream, work...
Just keep going!

ACTIVITY E. YOUR WRITING PROMPTS

My spectrum of rigid/focused thinking and setting goals

Use the following vocabulary prompts and questions to complete your worksheet and then write your own poems, thoughts, mini-stories or narrative for each topic below.

Word prompts

Rigid thinking: One-track mind, stuck, inflexible, anxious, particular, strict, perfectionist, precise, repetitive, detailed, focused, exact, accurate, fixed, set, unchanging, permanent, meticulous, specific.

Focused mind: Intense, passionate, achievement, goals, positive, driven, obsessed, motivated, single-minded, problem-orientated, constructive, powerful, forceful, dynamic, inspired, relentless, completion.

Event: When does this happen to me?

When do you find your thoughts get stuck? Does this affect particular areas of your life?

In what way does rigid or focused thinking affect daily activities? Are there times when your focused thinking is helpful?

Meaning: What does this mean for me?

Do you have a very black and white way of viewing events or people so they are maybe good or bad and no possibility of anything else can be considered?

Are you completely focused in a way that means other activities are pushed aside? Do you find that interruptions annoy you?

How is this thinking style beneficial to you? Are there any disadvantages to it?

Strategies: To help me change my thoughts I can:

What would motivate you to change thoughts that are not supporting you? Would a wide range of hobbies/interests help you to change your focus when needed?

Could you use your hyper-focus to ignore negative thoughts and achieve your dreams?

Goals: To help me achieve my goals I can:

Do you think your intense focus could support you when trying to achieve your goals?

Would it help to create a vision board to focus on related to your goals by collecting images and quotes and writing down your aims? Do you find it helpful to have deadlines to meet to get started and complete projects?

My spectrum of rigid/focused thinking and setting goals

Record your thoughts and experiences here.

Event: When does this happen to me?

My rigid thoughts get stuck on:	I am highly focused when:
•	•
•	•
•	•

Meaning: What does this mean for me?

_____

_____

Strategies: To help me change my thoughts I can:

_____

_____

Goals: To help me achieve my goals I can:

_____

_____

This section outlines Finn's experiences of being impulsive. It provides an example to write about how impulsivity presents in you.

Finn's spectrum of impulsivity

Event: When is Finn impulsive?

Finn is impulsive when: • *upset or angry about something.*	*Finn is not impulsive when:* • *speaking to new people* • *trying new food* • *trying new activities.*

Meaning: What does this mean for Finn?

Finn might have problems with: • *dealing with the consequences* • *managing her reactions* • *discovering new ways of doing things* • *socialising and travelling.*	*Finn might be good at:* • *saying what she thinks when angry* • *doing the same thing over and over and developing knowledge in that area.*

Strategies: Finn is able to stop and think when she:

- *takes a break to stop and monitor her actions or responses*
- *checks things through with someone she trusts to work out how she feels and how to respond appropriately.*

Finn's spectrum of impulsivity

Read Finn's creative writing. How does impulsivity affect Finn? Do you think her strategy would be effective?

Finn is impulsive/not impulsive

Speaking out loud
Anywhere at all
Never results in impulsive talk.
Unless I am feeling tremendously angry!!!
But most of the time I am not actually terribly impulsive.

Meaning for Finn

Angry words
Impulsively said
Can never disappear
Once spoken.

Finn's strategies to stop and think

Ask 3 Questions – 3Qs

- Count to ten: Pause   What am I doing?

- Count another ten: Pause   What will this mean for me tomorrow?

- Count another ten: Pause   What will this mean for other people?

ACTIVITY G. YOUR WRITING PROMPTS

My spectrum of impulsivity

Use the following vocabulary prompts and questions to complete your worksheet and then write your own poems, thoughts, mini-stories or narrative for each topic below.

Word prompts

Impulsive: Quick, spontaneous, excitement, exhilaration, thrill, rash, reckless, discovery, unexpected, unplanned, hasty, consequences, mistake, penalty, regrets, accidental, impromptu, unintended, irresponsible, uncontrolled, unforeseen, unpredictable.

Event: When am I impulsive?

I am impulsive when:

In what ways are you impulsive at home, school and/or with friends? Do you do things without thinking to try to fit in with friends? Do you find that being impulsive can mean you make hasty decisions?

I am not impulsive when:

What do I never rush into? Why do I not act impulsively over some things?

Meaning: What does this mean for me?

I might have problems with:

What do you think could happen if you are impulsive? Would it be a positive or negative thing to be impulsive? Are you good at predicting what will happen next? How might impulsivity affect your relationships?

I might be good at:

What are the benefits of being quick to act? How could being impulsive support you in achieving or discovering things?

Strategies: I am able to stop and think when I:

Could you have a routine that you follow any time you suspect you might act impulsively – playing a game on your phone to have thinking time? Would a quick bullet point list help you focus your mind on what is happening? How about keeping a journal to record occasions when you tend to be impulsive?

ACTIVITY H. MY WORKSHEET

My spectrum of impulsivity

Record your thoughts and experiences here.

Event: When am I impulsive?

I am impulsive when:	I am not impulsive when:
•	•
•	•
•	•

Meaning: What does this mean for me?

I might have problems with:	I might be good at:
•	•
•	•
•	•

Strategies: I am able to stop and think when I:

_____

_____

_____

_____

This section provides a summary of Finn's executive functioning profile. Read through it and use all the information you have learnt about your spectrum of executive functioning throughout this chapter to create your own version.

What's Finn's spectrum of executive functioning?

Finn's executive functioning strengths:

- *Dependable long-term memory useful for exam revision.*

- *Able to remember stuff in detail from a long time ago.*

- *Super-detailed focus means she notices things that no one else would ever see.*

- *Hyper-focuses to get things done, stays focused on one aim and achieves her goals.*

- *Capable of attaining whatever she decides to do as being unable to stop can be very useful.*

- *Consistent positive thoughts can generate endless motivation.*

- *Relentless focus means she will not give up until she finishes what she set out to do.*

Finn's executive functioning challenges:

- *Her ability to keep organised with practical tasks needs support.*

- *Gets overwhelmed with minor tasks.*

- *Can't start, then can't stop.*

- *Instantly forgetting or muddling up things that she has just heard. This is very annoying!*

- *Finds it impossible to follow verbal instructions.*

- *Thoughts get stuck and it can be hard to change them.*
- *Rigid negative thoughts can become a habit and that gradually take over.*

Finn would like other people to know:

- *how to recognise that executive functioning causes her lots of stress and she has a lot of stuff going on here*
- *how to understand that some things are genuinely harder for her*
- *how to make allowances when she is disorganised, confused and can't start or stop*
- *how to give her extra time and consideration for the things she finds hard*
- *how to suggest strategies but let her choose what works best for her.*

What's my spectrum of executive functioning?

Record your thoughts and experiences here.

My executive functioning strengths:

_____

_____

_____

_____

My executive functioning challenges:

_____

_____

_____

_____

I would like other people to know:

_____

_____

_____

_____

What's Finn's spectrum of executive functioning?

Read Finn's creative writing and consider what similarities or differences you have compared with Finn's profile of executive functioning.

Dear people

I live in a bit of a muddle
I'm always slightly befuddled
This disorganised clutter
It seems to multiply daily.
As for prioritisation, well that's another complication.
You know that it's true that this mess is only going to get worse.
Some things just need to reside in chaotic disorder
Most of the time I have to say
It's quite alright by me
    Until I think of a sort of plan
To get me far away from the jumble of things waiting and waiting...
I might just make some totally impulsive decision
To avoid thinking too much about all this stuff
As my head is already full to capacity with all this
information I can never seem to forget
I remember it well, for no particular reason, exactly what was said in 1999
Every fact and detail, and you can be sure I am right!
But it seems I have no memory at all for what you just said thirty seconds ago!
Now I must get back to my favourite point of my focus
With this incredibly close attention to detail and repetitive rigid thought patterns
Making my aims 100% vividly clear
Nothing will stop me from achieving anything I set my mind to
With my relentless single-minded pursuit of my goals and targets
Motivation training is not a requirement
I know without any reservation
I can reach any goal in my life
Which is undoubtedly my single greatest strength!!

What's my spectrum of executive functioning?

Record your poems, thoughts or mini-stories here.

Why don't you write a poem or a story about:

- your executive functioning strengths

- your executive functioning challenges

- what you would like other people to know about your spectrum of executive functioning?

_____

_____

_____

_____

_____

_____

_____

_____

_____

_____

ACTIVITY K. MY PROFILE CHART

My executive functioning profile

Strengths	Challenges
•	•
•	•
•	•
•	•
•	•

Strategies	Goals
•	•
•	•
•	•
•	•

Top three things you need to know about me

•

•

•

Chapter 2

Know Your Spectrum of Sensory Things

Introduction

Sensory experiences cover a range of areas which can be divided into sensory sensitivities, sensory integration, interoception system and sensory synaesthesia.

Sensory sensitivities: Sounds/smells/taste/vision

Sensory sensitivity means we are more or less sensitive to everything around us. It affects our hearing, vision, smell and taste. If we are under-sensitive we may not notice lots of things such as noises, pain or changes in temperature and we may not have the expected reactions to those things. When we are over-sensitive it means we experience sensory information more intensely than other people, leading to reactions that seem to be disproportionate to what is actually happening.

Loud noises can hurt our ears as we hear the sounds more loudly than other people, and this can be very painful and frightening, especially if it is a sudden sound. Whereas other people will filter out irrelevant noises allowing them to focus on someone speaking, we might find it difficult to block out background noises, so we will hear every sound in a room all at once at the same volume, which can be loud and overwhelming. We can also have problems distinguishing between sounds as they get distorted within our sensory channels and this can cause irritation or pain. It might almost feel as if the noise is assaulting our ears and skin.

Smells or tastes can be overpowering and might make us feel ill, or we may not notice them. Visual sensitivities can mean that fluorescent lights, especially those that flicker, can cause headaches and tiredness. If bright lights affect us, we might have difficulty getting to sleep even with only a narrow chink of light shining through, as it distracts us and we just can't settle until it is covered over. Issues with visual processing mean that objects at the side of our vision might become magnified and be really distracting for us but other people won't even notice them, while objects that are straight ahead might be blurred and we can't see them very well (National Autistic Society (NAS) 2016). This process can also happen the other way around with blurred vision of objects to the side and those directly in front of us appearing much bigger (NAS 2016). This can make direct eye contact uncomfortable and even painful due to feelings of sensory overload and we might need to avoid meeting people's gaze. Visual distortions can happen when reading or working on computers, meaning that the words are blurred or jump around and our eyes tire more quickly; this is called Irlen's Syndrome.

Sensory integration

Sensory integration allows our brains to process and organise the various sensations that we feel. This relates to our senses in three areas: tactile integration, proprioceptive system and vestibular system (NAS 2016).

Tactile integration: Touch/pain/pressure/temperature/texture

Tactile integration means how we experience touch, pain, temperature, texture and pressure (NAS 2016). Our skin can be more or less sensitive to touch. We can find a light touch painful or not feel any pain at all. Sometimes we need lots of pressure on our body to make us feel relaxed and this can help us sleep too.

Temperatures may affect our bodies differently so we don't feel the cold or heat in relation to our environment. This means that we might not wear the appropriate clothes for different seasons as our body's temperature system has its own thermostat.

The texture of food and material can be uncomfortable and sometimes difficult for us to cope with. This can lead us to have a very restricted diet because we like or dislike certain foods. It might be hard for us to eat food if it is lumpy or chewy. Labels on clothes can be itchy or painful, whereas harsh, thick materials might hurt or irritate our skin.

These heightened experiences of our senses are invisible, but they can be extreme, resulting in pain and distress. This can lead to over-reactions that seem inappropriate to those who don't have these kinds of sensory experiences with their tactile integration.

Proprioceptive system: Body awareness

The second group related to sensory integration involves our proprioception system, which sends messages to our brains to let us know how to position our bodies so we can move or sit. The signals from the body about how to move and carry out the movements may not be understood by our brain. This means our awareness of our body can be under-sensitive and we can have problems locating our body's position within our surroundings. We are not able to automatically work out where our body begins and ends. This could cause us to have an odd posture or stand too close to someone, bump into things, fall off a chair or be clumsy, and we might find it tricky to use cutlery and do up buttons (NAS 2016).

These various difficulties in understanding where our body is in relation to our surroundings might mean we don't want to take part in new activities as they are harder for us to learn and follow (NAS 2016).

Vestibular system: Body position/balance/sensory avoidance/stimulation

The final category of sensory integration is our vestibular system. This refers to our body's sense of balance which allows us to co-ordinate our movements and work out changes in our head's position (NAS 2016). We might find it difficult to control our limbs, take part in activities that require balance, start or stop when running, keep a bike cycling straight or cope with motion when travelling. Our bodies can't sense how to move around and make judgements about space and distance in relation to our position (NAS 2016).

When we have an oversensitive vestibular system we may avoid sensory experiences that we find scary because it is harder for us to sense our body position and the space around us (NAS 2016). We might get scared when getting on and off escalators or stepping down from a kerb as it could seem like a great height, or keeping our balance when walking on uneven surfaces might mean we have a tendency to trip over (NAS 2016).

If we have an under-sensitive vestibular system then we tend to seek out sensory stimulation as it makes us feel good. Often activities like spinning, bouncing, rocking or swinging can be very soothing. These repetitive movements help us to regulate our bodies, making us feel calm (NAS 2016).

Interoception system

Our interoception system allows our bodies to understand internal sensations so we can work out when we are feeling hungry, tired, sick or afraid and we can know that we are in pain (Greutman 2017). With autism, our interoception system can be less or more sensitive to the internal sensations in our bodies (Greutman 2017). If we are under-sensitive this means we might not notice that we are hungry or realise we are tired. Or we may experience pain or distress because we are overwhelmed with sensations if we are over-sensitive.

Sensory synaesthesia

Synaesthesia means that we receive information through one sensory system which then leaves through another. For example, we might hear a number or word and experience it as a colour, or we could visualise patterns with certain concepts, such as imagining the days of the weeks as a spiral (University of Sussex 2017).

Pain, taste and smells can create colours or images in our minds so that hearing some food names can generate the taste and texture in our mouths as if we are eating it (US 2017). We may experience synaesthesia through several sensory channels at once, with a word seen as a pattern, felt as a shape and tasting like a food all at once (Bogdashina 2016). If we see someone else being touched we can feel like we are being touched the same way (Bogdashina 2016) and our emotions can trigger colours or sensations in our bodies.

All these unusual sensations might cause a lot of confusion and they could lead to sensory overload (Bogdashina 2016), so it is important that we learn to recognise and understand them. We can also use this information to become more aware of our feelings.

Individual sensory experiences

We can have a sensory fascination with particular smells, lights, textures, tastes or movements like spinning, jumping, touching certain textures or looking at shiny objects which can give us a lot of pleasure (Bogdashina 2016).

We experience sensory stimuli in these different ways, because the sensory messages in our bodies get mixed up, so our reactions and behaviour are different to other people. We can experience hyper (over) or hypo (under) sensitivities in one or two of the areas described, or in all of them. These sensory sensitivities can be present all the time or they can come and go. Sometimes they can be really strong, having a significant effect on us, and then they may become quite mild within minutes, days or over years. The intensity of how we experience these feelings may vary depending on many factors including tiredness, overwhelm and stress.

How our bodies process sensory information can affect our experiences of the world and this can be difficult to cope with. Routines and familiar environments can become really important to us as they help us to gain some feeling of control over the outside world when we have so many factors affecting us.

A lot of these sensory experiences happen beneath the surface so no one else can see what we are going through and this makes it hard for other people to understand us. We might have unusual responses or behaviours that don't make sense and this can cause a lot of judgement. As other people don't experience the world the way we do, they can't really understand unless we explain what is happening underneath.

When we are overwhelmed by sensory information it can lead to us having a shutdown or a meltdown. At this stage we might not be able to communicate our needs or what is affecting us.

If we find out what our sensory profile is, then we can gradually learn to develop strategies to deal with anything that causes us problems to reduce the impact on us.

This will also help other people to understand our behaviours and reactions better so they can get a greater appreciation of what sensory differences in autism mean, and in turn this will allow them to support us when necessary.

This section outlines Finn's various sensory sensitivity experiences. It can be used as a template to work out your own spectrum of sensory sensitivities.

Finn's spectrum of sensory sensitivities: Sounds/smells/taste/vision

Activity: How do different sounds affect Finn?

- *The nerves in her ears shiver in time with the tiniest of crunches made by teeth close by. Also known as 'Misophonia'.*

- *Her mind feels like it will explode with too many noises attacking her.*

- *The tiniest of sounds repeating all the time drill pockets of stress deep into her head.*

- *Can't stand the sound of rattling coins or keys.*

- *Loves the sound of really loud music.*

Activity: How does Finn experience different smells and tastes?

- *Too many fish smells overpower her – only one option left, get out fast.*

- *Loves the smell of paper in new books.*

- *No problem with any tastes and loves the taste of chocolate!!!*

Activity: What visual sensitivities does Finn have?

- *The white glaring computer screen blares into her watering eyes, making it hard to work for a long time.*

- *Her eyes get distracted by something really tiny that no one else would notice and it drives her crazy!*

- *Loves to watch sunlight shimmering through the leaves of a tree.*

Finn's spectrum of sensory sensitivities: Sounds/smells/taste/vision

Read Finn's creative writing. Does Finn experience hyper- or hypo-reactions to different sensory input?

Sounds

The tiniest of noises
Creeping up through the floor boards
Create an intense kind of irritation.

When one noise is combined
With three or more sounds
I am heading toward
A very quick shutdown.

Smells

I can't stand the smell of fish!!!

Taste

Chocolate...it's all mine!!!!!!!

Visual

Computer screen glare makes my tired eyes struggle to read and absorb the information. I have to switch the image to a slightly shaded pink that makes all the words so much easier to read. But when I am outside I can stand under the biggest tree and follow the movements of the sunlight glistening through the leaves above for ever such a long time.

ACTIVITY A. YOUR WRITING PROMPTS

My spectrum of sensory sensitivities: Sounds/smells/taste/vision

Use the following vocabulary prompts and questions to complete your worksheet and then write your own poems, thoughts, mini-stories or narrative for each topic below.

Activity: How do different sounds affect me?

Word prompts

Sound: Agitate, piercing, pain, shiver, explode, stressed, thundering rolls, smashing, antagonise, overwhelmed, sharp, intense, concentrated, acute, stabbing, knife-like, screech, prickle, writhe, wriggle, soothing, calm, repetitive, tranquil, intense, loud, comforting, restful, gentle, uplifting.

How do you react to loud noises? Do you get distracted by tiny sounds that no one else notices? Does your head feel like it will explode when there are too many sounds? Are there certain noises that you really enjoy listening to? If so, what are they and why do you like them?

Activity: How do I experience different smells and tastes?

> # Word prompts
>
> **Smells/taste:** Sublime, tasty, enjoyable, seek out, satisfying, crave, inhale, savour, agreeable, sensational, fishy, perfumes, fragrance, un/pleasant, body products, odour, stink, offensive, spicy, burning, food, gasping, retching, sick, overpowering, pale, shun, evade, uncontrollable, all-consuming, intense, grimace, reject, refusal, disgusting, food separation, strong, overpowering.

Are there certain tastes or smells that you seek out? Why do you like these?

Do you avoid perfumes, deodorants or certain food smells? When eating do you prefer each bit of food to be separate on your plate so they don't touch?

Activity: What visual sensitivities do I have?

> # Word prompts
>
> **Vision:** Blurred, squinty, hurt, fuzzy, overload pain, irritation, dizzy, sick, weak, tiredness, headache, migraine, distorted, disorientation, harsh, stressed, discomfort, intensity, shiny, sparkly, flashing, glittery, gleaming, iridescent, reflecting, shimmering, movement, colours.

How does the glare from computer screens affect your eyes? Do you get headaches from fluorescent lights? Will small objects distract you while everything straight ahead seems blurred? Is direct eye contact painful?

Do you love to watch lights flickering? What sort of lights do you find interesting to watch?

ACTIVITY B. MY WORKSHEET

My spectrum of sensory sensitivities

Record your thoughts and experiences here.

Activity: How do different sounds affect me?

_____

_____

_____

_____

Activity: How do I experience different smells and tastes?

_____

_____

_____

_____

Activity: What visual sensitivities do I have?

_____

_____

_____

_____

This section outlines Finn's sensory integration experiences. It can be followed for support in identifying your own experience of sensory integration.

Finn's spectrum of tactile integration:
Touch/pain/pressure/temperature/texture

Finn's experience of touch and pain:

- She loves to touch different types of materials or objects anywhere she goes.

- No over- or under-sensitivities to pain.

Finn's experience of pressure:

- Tired eyes close over but her body restlessly lies awake. She needs to be wrapped in a cocoon of blankets to sleep well.

- Tense bones + stressed mind = deep pressure relief time.

- When she brushes her hair ten times in a row it's only because it makes her head feel great. It's so intense, beauty never comes into it.

Finn's experience of temperature:

- When everyone else is wrapped up she might be happy in a T-shirt.

Finn's experience of texture:

- Seven hours of the same clothes makes her skin shriek with a relentless kind of constrictive irritation, until she can change into clothes that have a different feel to them. Then she can relax!

- Labels irritate but not as much as they used to.

- Wobbly jelly, lumpy custard served cold...oh no, no, no, no, no!!!!!

Finn's spectrum of tactile integration:
Touch/pain/pressure/temperature/texture

Read Finn's creative writing. How does Finn experience these different tactile sensations? Could these various factors be useful or cause her any problems?

Touch

Trailing finger tips along the cold metal railings, purposely walking over raised path markings, rubbing certain materials between my fingers, sweeping my hand over any kind of sculpture.

Pressure

I love to be compressed until all the stress seeps out of my pores with endless blankets on top, pressing me down allowing my bones to stretch until I feel fantastically relaxed.

Temperature

Hot or cold
Rain or snow
Mixed-up weather sense
Equals some unusual seasonal clothes.

Texture

Chewy, stringy, oily fish.
Greasy soaked bacon or steak
Shrivel me up inside.
I feel sick!!

ACTIVITY C. YOUR WRITING PROMPTS

My spectrum of tactile integration:
Touch/pain/pressure/temperature/texture

Use the following vocabulary prompts and questions to complete your worksheet and then write your own poems, thoughts, mini-stories or narrative for each topic below.

My experience of touch and pain:

Word prompts

Touch and pain: Ache, aggravating, burning, stabbing, throbbing, irritation, unbearable, excruciating, gentle, rough, firm, avoidance, lack of sensitivity, hyper-sensitivity, contorted, acute, scowl, grimace, frown.

What types of touch do you find hard to deal with? When do you find touch more or less difficult to cope with?

Do you seem to experience pain differently to other people? Do people think you overreact or show no reaction? How does pain feel in your body?

My experience of pressure:

Word prompts

Pressure: Force, weight, heaviness, anxiety/pain release, de-stress, decompress, sleep, switch-off, deep relaxation, squeeze, hug, press, feel complete/satisfied, happy, safe, secure, protected, sheltered.

Does the sensation of having a heavy weight on your body help you relax? What do you use to create this feeling? When do you find this pressure helpful?

My experience of temperature:

Word prompts
Temperature: Hot, cold, icy, burn, tepid, warm, shiver, high, low, humid, distinguish.

Do you not notice the cold in winter and choose to wear summer clothes? Or do you find that you wear warm, winter clothes, even when the weather is hot outside?

My experience of texture:

Word prompts
Texture: Jagged, prickly, rough, paper, fragile, lumpy, chewy, grimace, frown, tough, rubbery, stringy, gristly, leathery, material, scratchy, boa constrictor, razor-sharp, intolerable.

Are there any foods that you really struggle to cope with eating, such as lumps or chewy, stringy textures? What about the feeling of certain materials on your skin?

ACTIVITY D. MY WORKSHEET

My spectrum of tactile integration:
Touch/pain/pressure/temperature/texture

Record your thoughts and experiences here.

My experience of touch and pain:

_____

_____

_____

My experience of pressure:

_____

_____

_____

My experience of temperature:

_____

_____

_____

My experience of texture:

_____

_____

_____

This section outlines Finn's experiences of sensory integration. It can be used as a template to work out your own profile of sensory integration.

Finn's spectrum of sensory integration

Proprioceptive system: Body awareness

Finn's experiences of body awareness and knowing how to move:

- Sometimes her body stands a little too close for the other person's comfort but this doesn't happen too often.

- Exercise routines are impossible to follow as she can't work out which arm to put where, so she can get into a total muddle.

- Bruises and bumps sometimes seem to have a magnetic attraction to her body as she can't always automatically work out where she begins and ends.

- She loves to wear hoods as they make her head feel sheltered and enclosed, she can feel her head close to her body instead of the never-ending wide open space all around.

Finn's spectrum of sensory integration

Proprioceptive system: Body awareness

Read Finn's creative writing. How does body awareness affect Finn? Have you experienced these kinds of things?

Finn's body awareness

Doors
Cupboards   =   Bruises!!
Tables
Chairs

Finn's ability to move

Aerobics
Tone your body
Flatten your abs
Lift your butt
Or make you fall over trying to negotiate impossible
instructions with your terribly misdirected legs...

Oh, just let me go home!!!

Why did I bother!!

Finn loves to use her body to:

- get rid of difficult feelings of anger.

Vestibular system: Body position/balance/ sensory avoidance/stimulation

Finn's experiences of body position and balance:

- She is able to work out her head position and control her body movements.
- On car journeys she can sometimes get sick.

Finn wants to avoid these movements:

- No issues with sensory avoidance.

Finn loves to use her body to:

- rock from side to side without even realising she is doing it
- draw patterns with her pen, circles and triangles, shapes inside shapes, bring a quiet calm to her mind
- make weird, distorted shapes, with her arms twisting out all her stress
- swim and cycle as fast as she can, which makes her feel terrific inside
- getting deep pressure through surrounding herself in blankets helps her to sleep.

Vestibular system: Body position/balance/ sensory avoidance/stimulation

Read Finn's creative writing. What way does Finn move and use her body? How are you similar or different?

Finn's balance

Travelling by car leads to sickness caused by the constant motion of the vehicle affecting my body balance inside. Reading a book might make it worse but keeping my head upright and looking straight in front always helps.

Finn's use of her body

I find myself sitting on my own and I suddenly realise I am rocking to and fro with a systematic rhythm that makes my body smooth and warm. Then when I am very, very angry I feel an intense need to thump and hit my body up against walls which releases all that pent-up anger from deep inside.

Happy and calm

*Hibernate
Under my bed clothes
With twenty sheets
I won't need to count sheep!*

ACTIVITY E. YOUR WRITING PROMPTS

My spectrum of sensory integration

Proprioceptive system: Body awareness

Use the following vocabulary prompts and questions to complete your worksheet and then write your own poems, thoughts, mini-stories or narrative for each topic below.

My experiences of body awareness and knowing how to move:

Word prompts

Body awareness: Confusion, unaware, space, clumsy, ungainly, awkward, body sense, stance, trip, co-ordination, movement, direction, posture, slanted, sloped, unbalanced, distance, judgement, sense, crash, press, falling, tumbling, kicking, pressing.

Do you find it hard to know how close to stand next to someone else? Can you sense where your body starts and ends? Or do you have trouble locating your mouth when eating?

Can you start and stop easily when running or moving? Are you able to judge your movements when jumping or taking a step? Do you often fall off chairs for no reason? How well can your body copy or follow instructions in PE? When you are standing, does your body posture seem a bit unbalanced? Do you love to push and pull or crash against things or make yourself fall on purpose?

Vestibular system: Body position/balance/ sensory avoidance/stimulation

Use the following vocabulary prompts and questions to complete your worksheet and then write your own poems, thoughts, mini-stories or narrative for each topic below.

My experiences of body position and balance:

Word prompts

Balance: Falling, stumbling, lost in space, co-ordination, movement, poise, equilibrium, stability, motion, steadiness, dizzy, faltering, awkward, confused, hesitant, unsure, flailing, wobble, vertigo, disorientated, spin, rock, jump, impact, intensity, force, satisfaction, boredom.

Do you think you have a good sense of co-ordination to move your body with ease? Are you aware of where your head is or does it seem to be separate from your body? Can you ride a bike? How do you find changing directions or stopping and starting when running? Do you often get sick on car journeys? Would you spend lots of time on a trampoline or enjoy jumping down from heights? Do you like to rock or spin?

I want to avoid these movements:

Word prompts

Sensory avoidant behaviour: Clumsy, fearful, frightened, reassurance, support, avoidance, tears, pain, unknown, unable to gauge, judge, estimate, heights, distance, gaps, safe, danger.

What types of movement do you not like to do? Why do you find this hard? Is distance hard to judge when moving your body? Do wide, open spaces make you feel overwhelmed?

I love to use my body to:

Word prompts

Sensory-seeking behaviour: Spin, rock, push, press, weight, bang, circles, patterns, tip toes, jumping, hitting, twirling, twisting, revolving, repetitive movements, loud music, biting, scratching, bouncing, rhythmic, comfort, soothe, releasing, fingers, lights, textures, sounds.

What movements make you feel good? Do you like to rock, jump, spin, clap, stamp? Do you follow certain patterns of movement as part of a ritual? When do you use these types of movements?

ACTIVITY F. MY WORKSHEET

My spectrum of sensory integration

Record your thoughts and experiences here.

My experiences of body awareness and knowing how to move:

....

....

....

My experiences of body position and balance:

....

....

....

I want to avoid these movements:

....

....

....

I love to use my body to:

....

....

....

This section outlines Finn's experiences in relation to interoception and synaesthesia. You can use it as an example to help you to write about how these sensory differences present in your body and mind.

Finn's spectrum of interoception and sensory synaesthesia

Finn's interoception system gets confused when she:

- *doesn't realise she is hungry and tired and then has an unexpected shutdown*

- *ends up feeling very sick and overcome with exhaustion as she did too much work and didn't register when it was time to stop.*

How Finn experiences sensory synaesthesia:

- *Emotions form physical sensations within her body.*

- *Anger may be prickly spikes driving through her skin.*

- *Depression – a dense heavy weight pulling down her chest and over her skin.*

- *Sadness reacts with a heart flip at some upsetting thought.*

- *Happiness is a lightness in her body and a deep relaxation in her limbs.*

Finn's spectrum of interoception and sensory synaesthesia

Read Finn's creative writing. Think about how much awareness Finn has of what is happening in her body. Is she able to manage her body's needs effectively?

Finn's interoception system

Fixated attention leaves no chance of effective multi-tasking and food gets left waiting until I am ready to eat the whole fridge all at once!

Learning to find a balance between getting things done and working at a moderate pace has been an elusive goal for me so far in life. I don't expect it to change any time soon!

Finn's emotional synaesthesia

Whether upset or depressed, I might have no reactions on the surface but inside my body burns a deep blistering red as sharp thistles burst out from under my skin. My emotions paint pictures for me to understand them.

ACTIVITY G. YOUR WRITING PROMPTS

My spectrum of interoception and sensory synaesthesia

Use the following vocabulary prompts and questions to complete your worksheet and then write your own poems, thoughts, mini-stories or narrative for each topic below.

My interoception system gets confused when I:

Word prompts

Interoception system: Warnings, signals, signs, indicators, changes, alerts, awareness, register, ignore, disregard, overlook, dismiss, subtle, sudden, slow, minor, significant, notice, unnoticed, fluctuations, alarms, responsiveness, sensitivity, receptors, gradual.

Ability to recognise: Hunger, sickness, tiredness, pain, needing the toilet.

Can you understand what the different sensations in your body mean? Do you have a good sense of when to eat, drink or stop doing something because you are tired? When you are in pain or hungry, will you become overwhelmed with the feelings or not really register them?

How I experience sensory synaesthesia:

Word prompts

Sensory synaesthesia: Numbers, words, food, smell, visual, auditory, tactile, touch, hear, taste, emotions, sequences, patterns, images, reaction, automatic, confused messages, jumbled, disconnections, mixed-up connections, links, sensory channels, vivid, unusual, internal, instant, alternative processing, puzzled, perplexed, baffling, unconventional, bizarre, remarkable.

When you see someone else being touched will you feel the same sensation on your body? When too much is happening do you become overloaded, leading to confused sensory reactions?

Do you get unusual sensations in your body which seem to be related to your emotions?

When you hear a word will you experience it as a physical reaction, so 'ice-cream' leads to brain freeze? Or do you find that patterns form in your mind in response to particular words?

ACTIVITY H. MY WORKSHEET

My spectrum of interoception and sensory synaesthesia

Record your thoughts and experiences here.

My interoception system gets confused when I:

_____

_____

_____

_____

_____

How I experience sensory synaesthesia:

_____

_____

_____

_____

_____

This section summarises Finn's overall sensory profile. Read it through and then fill in your worksheet to create your own version using all the different things we have covered in the chapter.

What's Finn's spectrum of sensory things?

Finn's heightened sensory experiences:

- *Repetitive noises: tap, tap, tap like a chisel burrowing into her brain. Loud music is always good, with the song of the moment on constant repeat!*

- *Computer screen glare and tiny objects off to the side irritate far too much!*

- *Loves trees with sunlight breaking through.*

- *Cold railings to run her fingers along, press her feet onto those bumps in the road.*

- *Exhaustion envelops, her body collapses, she needs deep pressure input to de-stress and chill out.*

- *Hot in winter, cold in summer, mixed-up clothes, she dresses according to her body temperature.*

- *Lumpy, jelly, chewy, smelly fishy foods don't mix well for her, but chocolate forever!*

- *Moving her body to follow instructions in co-ordinated ways is tricky to do.*

- *Doesn't always know where her body ends and begins, so hoods are always good.*

- *Temporary confusion in her sense of balance means that car journeys could lead to stomach strife!*

- *Not recognising when to stop working, eat or when she is getting too tired.*

- *Emotions processed through her body help her make sense of life events.*

Finn is OK with these sensory experiences:

- Lights or an average level of sound.
- Tastes and most smells are fine.
- Understanding her head and body position.
- Feeling pain.

To feel good Finn needs to:

- manage noises, especially unnecessary ones like adverts which only ever annoy!
- withdraw when tired, overloaded and unable to function properly
- use different ways to make her feel deep sensory pressure input any time it is required
- rock back and forth, drawing repetitive patterns with her finger or pen to bring a sort of calming energy
- understand what different sensations mean about her emotions.

Finn would like other people to know that:

- sensory issues can be mild one day and severe the next
- tiredness and stress make them worse
- deep pressure of any kind can be very calming
- lots of little things that do no harm bring her a sense of peace and satisfaction
- her different way of processing the external world leads to different reactions
- sensory sensitivities are more than being fussy!

What's my spectrum of sensory things?

Record your thoughts and experiences here.

My heightened sensory experiences:

_____

_____

_____

I am OK with these sensory experiences:

_____

_____

_____

To feel good I need to:

_____

_____

_____

I would like other people to know that:

_____

_____

_____

What's Finn's spectrum of sensory things?

Read Finn's creative writing and consider what similarities or differences you have with Finn's sensory profile.

Finn's heightened sensory experiences

A repetitive noise begins to tap against my brain,
grating into my cells, driving me insane!
With these voices in a room, a TV blasting out too,
it becomes intense, my head compresses.
It closes tight into a pressure vault. Ready to explode!! Watch out...
But give me some endlessly loud music, well that's no problem at all!
Except for those who wonder about her contradictory behaviour...
While moving my body and following instructions do not work out well, not one little bit!!
Then these emotions cause a commotion as they swirl inside my body.
Let me rock back and forth for a short while, they
will settle down with this simple pastime.
Sometimes these things are very intense and other
times they don't have such a big impact.
It all depends on too many things to fit in here!!

Finn feels good...

Limit noises
Turn adverts down.

Listen to one voice at a time.
Avoid trifle and table corners!

Rhythmic rocking, instant calm
Squashed beneath deep pressure, it feels just GREAT!!
Pay attention!! To warning signals in my body...
Before it is too late!!!

Dear people

Autism is a spectrum of various sensitivities
Changes occur apparently randomly throughout each day.
Tired or stressed these sensory things will all become worse.
Full of ambiguities that people don't seem to understand
Multiple noises agitate...but loud music I love it really loud!
My reactions are different and often may seem a bit bizarre
Though I can assure you quite confidently it really is quite normal for me.
It's not being fussy to have a different way of experiencing this world!

ACTIVITY J. MY WORKSHEET

What's my spectrum of sensory things?

Record your poems, thoughts or mini-stories here.

Why don't you write a poem or a story about:

- your sensory sensitivities

- sensory factors that don't affect you

- what you would like other people to know about your spectrum of sensory things?

_____

_____

_____

_____

_____

_____

_____

_____

_____

ACTIVITY K. MY PROFILE CHART

My sensory profile

Sensitivities	What's OK?
•	•
•	•
•	•
•	•
•	•

Strategies

•

•

•

•

•

Top three things you need to know about me

•

•

•

Chapter 3

Know Your Spectrum of Processing Differences

Introduction

Autism means that we may process information differently to other people. Our ability to process all the different noises, words, images, actions or activities around us can change according to circumstances and over time. This means that we might be able to absorb and understand everything happening around us one day, but another time our processing skills might not work effectively enough for us to make sense of everything. Processing differences can be related to how our brains work in terms of central coherence and the influence of sensory factors on how we perceive the world.

Central coherence

Central coherence is a term for being able to use our experiences and turn them into a story that helps us to make sense of the world (Delfos 1998). Our natural focus tends to see the details and all the separate parts of a conversation, task or situation. We can spot things which most people will miss, but we might have trouble putting all this knowledge together in our minds so that we can use it to understand what to say or do. Other people's form of central coherence means that they will see the whole story or image, rather than the details, and be able to process it all at once, so they automatically know how to act in a certain situation even if they have never dealt with it before.

It provides an internal guide to everyday life that other people will not have to think about. Whereas if we tend to see all the parts then it is much harder to understand what is happening, work out what to think about it, say or do and predict what will happen next. At the same time, we can also be really good at seeing the whole picture all at once. We might find it easy to see all the different parts of a situation and then put them together in a way that is really detailed and covers every single aspect arranged in perfect order. Most people won't be able to perceive so much information; this allows us to have a very unique perspective of the world, which is a strength.

This form of processing can also mean that we perceive the physical world in fragments. This can be a way of coping with the information overload that results from absorbing everything around us all at once and having trouble breaking the whole into parts (Bogdashina 2016). Our minds automatically focus on smaller bits to allow us to understand them, though we can't put these pieces together to make sense of them. This means that we might recognise someone by their hair rather than their whole face, and if the hairstyle changes even slightly then we might not know who the person is. This is called prosopagnosia (Bogdashina 2016).

Sensory factors and processing experiences

When our senses are overwhelmed then this might cause us to begin to process information differently. We might be triggered for various reasons, including when we are under stress, tired and unable to cope (Bogdashina 2016). There are several types of experiences we can have when our processing skills are finding it hard to cope, including shutdowns, mono-processing and delayed processing.

Processing shutdown

We can have problems filtering incoming information through our different senses; everything we see, hear, feel, taste and smell might be processed all at once by our bodies and minds (Bogdashina 2016). Our senses can't sort out what bits of information are important to look at or listen to and what we can ignore. Then our minds get overwhelmed at having to deal with too much information and we may have a partial or a complete shutdown or end up having a meltdown (Bogdashina 2016). Other people can filter out background noises and focus on someone speaking, but we might hear every noise in the room and not be able to concentrate, or it may even hurt our ears. When we are looking at someone it can be painful to have eye contact with so much other external information affecting us at the same time.

Mono-processing

Our minds adapt to help us process so much information by making sure we only think about or see one part of an object or situation at a time. This is called mono-processing (Bogdashina 2016). This reduces the amount of information being processed so that we can keep functioning, but we will only be absorbing a fraction of the necessary information. Another reaction may be that our sensory perceptions of people or events become fragmented and broken down into parts (Bogdashina 2016). However, when our brain breaks down this information so that we can cope with processing it, we have trouble recognising what these separate parts mean (Bogdashina 2016). We can't make sense of all these individual pieces of information to put them together to understand the whole situation, object or person and we will focus on one detail while missing lots of other things (Bogdashina 2016). This means that we might see someone's eyes, mouth or their hair but not actually know what their face looks like, meaning we are unable to recognise them out of a familiar context (Bogdashina 2016). If we are being spoken to, we might only be able to focus on the words and not process what is happening at the same time. These forms of mono-processing and fragmented processing mean that we are much slower to understand what is happening around us.

Delayed processing

We have to actively think through each piece of information we have heard, seen or felt and work it all out in sequence, one stage after the other, before we can fully appreciate the whole picture. This can mean that our understanding of what is going on around us and our reactions are delayed (Bogdashina 2016). We need more time to think about whatever we are going to say or do to be able to respond appropriately. This slower processing style might mean that we get left behind in conversations or activities; it can seem as if everyone else seems to know what to say or do while we are trying to put all these pieces together. This can be frustrating for us to have to deal with and confusing for other people to understand our responses or actions. These different processing experiences can be made even more difficult to cope with as we don't always automatically retain information that we have learnt.

Generalisation of our knowledge

All the information learnt from our previous experiences in conversations or everyday activities and jobs might not be retained for future use. Our minds don't apply the knowledge learnt from previous experiences when we have to deal with the same circumstances again even if everything is exactly the same (Bogdashina 2016). Our understanding of a situation only relates to that individual occasion. When we are presented with the same event again, it is as if we have never dealt with this before. This is because we have difficulty generalising our knowledge from one task to another (Bogdashina 2016). Information is not always absorbed by our brains in a way that we can use it again and we can't adapt what we do know to cope with slight changes. This means that our familiarity with a situation does not help us adjust our behaviour and react appropriately as it does for other people (Bogdashina 2016). We continually have to keep gathering all the separate parts together to recapture what we already figured out, no matter how many times we have coped with it before. Most people will acquire skills from their experiences which they can use again or adjust slightly to fit with a broader range of new demands. They develop an internal foundation from which they can speak and act effortlessly without having to think everything through for each individual occasion. Everyday situations that are easy and straightforward for most people can create a lot of work for us to keep up. Often these processing differences and other factors such as communication differences can mean that it is easier for us to copy other people's behaviours. But this could mean that we lose our sense of who we are and who we want to be.

Processing differences

It is important that we understand how we process information and the impact of sensory factors. By being aware of our internal experiences, we can make more sense of our processing style and then we can recognise what is happening to our bodies and minds. This will give us a greater chance of taking control of our responses and actions and help us to generalise what we have learnt for future situations. Over time, we can learn to act, speak and make decisions based on how we are processing information, rather than trying to copy other people and perhaps losing our own identity.

Experiencing the world in this way also means that we find it difficult to cope with changes (Bogdashina 2016). We enjoy routines and familiarity because we know what to expect and it helps to bring the outside world a little bit more under our control. Our internal experiences are invisible to other people and this means that our behaviours or interpretation of things can seem unusual to them.

Our processing style will be individual to us, so we could have a lot of differences in this area that happen regularly or we might only occasionally have minor differences in how we process information.

Developing our knowledge of how we process information will lead us to a greater sense of self-awareness, ensuring that we know how our minds work. It will also allow us to explain to others how these processing differences might present in us, such as why we are having trouble knowing what to say or when we are stressed by small changes to our routines. This will help us to be better understood and prevent misjudgements from occurring.

This section outlines Finn's experience of central coherence. It will help you to work out your own version of central coherence.

Finn's spectrum of central coherence

Event: What happened?

- *Finn found it hard to work out her opinion on a topic that she was studying as she was unable to put all the separate parts together, despite knowing lots of details about it.*

Reaction: What happened in Finn's body and mind?

- *Body tenses up as she cannot put any thoughts into words to respond appropriately.*

- *Blank mind due to nerves makes it even harder to think the topic through.*

- *Listens to other people's thoughts to copy what they say.*

Meaning: What does central coherence mean for Finn?

- *She sees most things as separate, unrelated parts, making it hard to put them all together into a conversation, opinion, action.*

- *Slow step-by-step thinking style that sees the importance of each detail.*

- *Eventually able to put things together but this takes extra time and effort.*

- *Embarrassment at being unable to gather her thoughts to create an opinion and say anything and anxious at being asked to speak.*

- *Frustration. She reads so much, but is still not able to grasp the whole topic and hold the separate parts in her mind all at once to develop her own viewpoint in discussions.*

Effect: How did other people react?

- Scornful at her inability to respond, asking 'Are you in the right lecture room?'

- Ignored her the next time topics were being discussed.

- Realised she was struggling to answer and carried on talking without any comment.

Strategies: What would support Finn's version of central coherence?

- Mind map of the facts, showing how they link up with opposing perspectives, listed in bullet points.

- Listening to lots of opinions so she can identify which she agrees with the most.

- Watching documentaries to give a holistic overview of important topics.

Finn's spectrum of central coherence

Read Finn's narrative. Can you recognise the experiences described?

I was studying for a degree in politics and even though I had read all the course books I was unable to talk about the topics as a whole in tutorials. I could see all the individual stories of things that had happened, but I could not take this information and turn it into a complete image of the political situations that I could then discuss. This made me feel very frustrated and nervous at having to talk in group discussions as I knew I would not be able to give an opinion like everyone else.

I try to use all my individual bits of knowledge to create mental templates that I can use to let me know what to do in each situation. But, when I have to have a new conversation, I might technically know how to speak and make eye contact, but that does not mean I can take the necessary sentences and create a conversation with the appropriate reactions and body language to perform socially. This means that conversations are a series of constantly random and unpredictable sentences and actions for me, rather than something familiar that I can easily adjust for different circumstances.

When presented with a task, I can complete the individual components, but I may not always see how they all fit together to complete the process. This means that I can end up not getting things done as my head will stop and either I don't know what to do or it will not occur to me to complete the next stage until something happens to make me understand or realise what I should have done. I can learn how to do things as a complete process, but I need to be taught in tiny steps until I can do things completely on my own.

At the same time, once I understand something really well I can take all the individual parts of a situation or topic and slowly piece them together in a systematic way, giving a very detailed overview that most people don't have.

Central coherence has a big effect on my perception and actions; this is further affected by my rigid thinking style, which means I get stuck on one thing and can't see beyond it.

ACTIVITY A. YOUR WRITING PROMPTS

My spectrum of central coherence

Use the following vocabulary prompts and questions to complete your worksheet and then write your own poems, thoughts, mini-stories or narrative for each topic below.

Word prompts

Central coherence: Spotlight, focus, detailed, perspective, parts, separate, individual, components, compartments, sections, detached, distinct, elements, stages, condensed, concentrated, compacted, miniscule, microscopic, delayed, slow, confused, unaware, holistic, global, broad, narrow, observe, copy, practice, anxiety, confidence, faces, object, recognise.

Event: What happened?

Think about a time when you had to understand a situation or conversation and take action. Did you find it easy to see all the parts of the situation, but hard to put them together to speak or take action? Or could you see exactly what needs to be done more clearly than everyone else? When would you notice both or one of these thinking styles happening?

Reaction: What happened in my body and mind?

What do you think about when presented with a situation that you are unsure of what to say or do? Is your mind blank in everyday situations? Do you feel nervous, frustrated or overwhelmed while other people just know what they should say or do?

Meaning: What does central coherence mean for me?

Do you find it confusing/frustrating that other people can work things out and automatically see how to do things or what to say? Is it difficult to cope with new situations as your mind does not always put things together to understand what to say or do? Do you perceive people or things in fragments and find it hard to work out who or what they are?

Do you want to take control and lead as you have such a good understanding of the whole situation or do you want to avoid things as you can never be sure you will know what to do?

Effect: How did other people react?

Are people impressed at your ability to see every tiny detail of each part or the whole task/situation? Do people think you are not very intelligent as you can't say anything or need to be told everything? Is your spotlight or global perspective thought to be positive or negative?

Strategies: What would support my version of central coherence?

Does systematically analysing the situation/task/topic provide you with a broader understanding of what to say or do? What helps you to understand things – observing and copying other people, making notes? Would it help if you had extra time to absorb the separate elements and put them together? Could your detailed and/or holistic perspective be useful in a particular job?

My spectrum of central coherence

Record your thoughts and experiences here.

Event: What happened?

_____

_____

_____

_____

Reaction: What happened in my body and mind?

_____

_____

_____

_____

Meaning: What does central coherence mean for me?

_____

_____

_____

_____

Effect: How do other people react?

_____

_____

_____

_____

Strategies: What would support my version of central coherence?

_____

_____

_____

_____

This section outlines Finn's experience of processing shutdowns. It can be used as a template to identify your own spectrum of processing shutdowns.

Finn's spectrum of processing shutdowns

Event: What happened?

Too much socialising and too many activities mean that Finn is exhausted. She can't think or function properly any more and she becomes unresponsive and cold and she has a very prickly reaction to other people.

Reaction: What happened in Finn's body and mind?

Body
Numbing exhaustion
Painfully tired, dragging
Can only mumble
No feelings
Auto-pilot
Heavy

Mind
Slow, foggy, blank, vague
Mono-processing, fragmented processing
Confused, distant, irritable
Disorientated, microscopic perspective
Unable to think or process situations
Unable to react quickly

Delayed reaction: What happened in Finn's body and mind afterwards?

Body
Sleepy
Painful skin

Weak
Slowly begins to speak again

Mind
Starts to think properly
Emotional reaction – annoyed at herself, embarrassed

Meaning: What did Finn's processing shutdown mean?

- Too tired to continue with any conversations or deal with social demands.

- She experiences social burnout faster than other people and needs to withdraw and have time alone.

- Slow, fragmented processing means she will not fully absorb conversations, situations.

Effect: How did other people react?

- Exasperation at her withdrawal and lack of communication or disgruntled responses.

- Gave her some time and space to get back to feeling OK.

- Left her out next time as they were so confused or angry at her unusual reactions.

- Did not notice anything unusual in her behaviour as she is always quiet and withdrawn.

Strategies: What would help Finn to deal with processing shutdowns?

- Developing an understanding of her warning signs that indicate she may be starting to shut down.

- Plan to avoid: Keep a journal of key triggers for when she will have a processing shutdown and how it can be prevented – noises, tiredness, socialising.

- Knowing when to withdraw from situations when she realises that she is beginning to shut down.

Finn's spectrum of processing shutdowns

Read Finn's creative writing. What effect do processing shutdowns have on Finn?

Event: What happened?

People exposure for far too long, total exhaustion quickly takes hold, words evaporate, thoughts disappear, the shutters go down, I am no longer available for comment. I'm done.

Finn's reactions

Too much happening
All around me
Means my sensory perceptions
Through my eyes, ears and skin
Start to shut down
Now I can see, hear, feel
Only one thing at a time.

Finn's delayed reaction

Curtains, blankets, solitude.
Tension slides away.
Tiredness slowly disappears.
As my body decompresses
With some time alone
I can start again.

Finn's processing shutdown

So many voices
I can't keep up.
Too many hours
Busy socialness hurts.
I thought I was OK.
But a sudden loss of energy
Means I can no longer cope
Or explain what is wrong.

Other people's reactions

People do not understand
Or give me time to recover.
I can't stop my reactions
I can't stop other people's perceptions.
Only those who want to understand
Will see who I am.

Finn's processing shutdown strategies

By working out what situations typically caused a shutdown I was able to gradually take control through monitoring how I felt and whether I should take part in something or not. When I could feel my body sinking and beginning to crash with lack of food, too much socialising or tiredness, I was able to start recognising when to go home. This helps to prevent any bad feelings from developing from other people and allows me to avoid getting into difficulties due to being unable to cope with the same amount as everyone else.

ACTIVITY C. YOUR WRITING PROMPTS

My spectrum of processing shutdowns

Use the following vocabulary prompts and questions to complete your worksheet and then write your own poems, thoughts, mini-stories or narrative for each topic below.

Word prompts

Body processing shutdown: Frozen, exhaustion, drained, numb, slowness, effort, weak, pain, prickly, barbed, spiky, bristly, aches and pains, heavy, fatigue, collapse, disintegrate, weariness, painful eye contact, speaking hurts, brain freeze, uncommunicative.

Mind processing shutdown: Irritation, slow, blank mind, speechless, wordless, withdrawn, confused, inhibited, remote, aloof, standoffish, introverted, solitary, quiet, unsociable, distant, engulfed, overcome, unthinking, stuck, bewildered, sullen, numbness.

Event: What happened?

What triggers caused the processing shutdown? Socialising, sensory overwhelm, lack of sleep or food, not enough time alone?

Reaction: What happened in my body and mind?

How does your mind feel when you can no longer think? Are you able to speak appropriately? What sensations do you feel in your body when you are unable to function properly? Can you keep working on autopilot or are you unable to do anything?

Delayed reaction: What happened in my body and mind afterwards?

How does your mind react as you begin to come out of the shutdown? Do you feel embarrassed, depressed or relieved? Does your body feel exhausted or reenergised and ready to start again?

Meaning: What did my processing shutdown mean?

What different factors might cause you to experience a processing shutdown? In what way will this impact on your life and those around you? What does this mean for your ability to cope with everyday life? How might a processing shutdown affect your personal safety?

Effect: How did other people react?

Did they notice you had stopped functioning properly? Were they supportive and understanding or annoyed/irritated at your lack of participation or reactions? Did they give you space to withdraw or pressurise you to participate?

Strategies: What would help me to deal with processing shutdowns?

Would it help to plan activities to ensure you can cope? What is most effective to allow you to recover – silence, space, music, exercise, food? How could you let other people know what is happening and how they could support you?

My spectrum of processing shutdowns

Record your thoughts and experiences here.

Event: What happened?

_____

_____

Reaction: What happened in my body and mind?

_____

_____

_____

_____

Delayed reaction: What happened in my body and mind afterwards?

_____

_____

_____

_____

Meaning: What did my processing shutdown mean?

_____

_____

_____

_____

_____

Effect: How did other people react?

_____

_____

_____

_____

Strategies: What would help me to deal with processing shutdowns?

_____

_____

_____

_____

This section outlines Finn's experience of delayed/mono-processing. It provides an example to help you identify your own spectrum of delayed/mono-processing.

Finn's spectrum of delayed/ mono–processing

Event: What happened?

- *Finn did not understand the conversation as there was too much noise which overwhelmed her and she had to switch her mind off to cope.*

Delayed reaction: What happened in Finn's body and mind after the event/conversation?

- *Repeats conversation to go through each part of it bit by bit to understand it as she was only absorbing one thing at a time and couldn't take it all in.*

- *Confusion about some parts of the conversation as they don't make sense and she will not get any hidden meanings and may have taken something literally.*

- *Felt bad because the other person thought she was being rude or didn't care as she did not respond as expected.*

Meaning: What did Finn's delayed/mono–processing mean?

- *Only figures out what she should have said after the event as she needs to take extra time to allow the information to be absorbed and analyse each aspect.*

- *She missed parts of the conversation which meant that her processing was delayed until much later when she suddenly realised what the person actually meant.*

- *Seems to be uncaring/uninterested/rude when she just didn't get the whole conversation or understand it straight away.*

Effect: How did other people react?

- *Made up their own interpretation of her responses.*

- *Thought she was rude because she did not react or say what they expected.*

- *Annoyed as she seemed to have no empathy for their story/perspective.*

Strategies: What strategies would support Finn's delayed/mono-processing?

- *Explain to other people that delayed/mono-processing could be affecting her understanding, responses and reactions.*

- *Ask questions to get alternative perspectives to identify if she has missed some aspects or not fully understood something.*

Finn's spectrum of delayed/ mono–processing

Read Finn's creative writing. How do you think delayed/mono-processing makes Finn feel?

What happened?

I did not understand the spoken words; it took a while to figure it all out, my processing style means I get left behind.

Finn's reactions

Conversation re-runs chattering loudly in my head
Leaves me puzzled over exactly what they meant.
It doesn't seem to make sense
I think I might have missed a bit.
Switched off my ears
To hear only parts of those words
Now I don't know what to think or say.

Finn's delayed/mono-processing

I am always the last to know
This leaves me feeling very low.
I can't keep up, I need to stop!
My head feels like it is going to explode!
I have to shut down these senses of mine.
Go into automatic self-protection mode.
Now I don't need to find out
What I didn't quite get
Once again!

Other people's reactions

As if!

She knew exactly what I meant!

How rude!

Finn's delayed/mono-processing strategies

Double check the facts	–	*question the meaning*
Discuss it, write it	–	*absorb the whole story*
Explain it, resolve it	–	*a note, text, poem*

ACTIVITY E. YOUR WRITING PROMPTS

My spectrum of delayed/mono-processing

Use the following vocabulary prompts and questions to complete your worksheet and then write your own poems, thoughts, mini-stories or narrative for each topic below.

Word prompts

Delayed/mono-processing: Slow, annoyed, infuriated, exasperated, confused, disadvantaged, rude, mistakes, puzzled, perplexed, baffled, misconstrued, bewildered, muddled, amusing, unusual, quirky, interesting, gradual, stages, mulling over, pondering, deliberating, methodical, details, separate parts, understanding.

Event: What happened?

Why were you experiencing delayed/mono-processing – noise, tiredness, shutdown, emotional overwhelm, seeing separate parts due to central coherence, not getting the hidden meaning, too many things to absorb all at once?

Reaction: What happened in my body and mind after the event/conversation?

How did it make you feel when you took longer to understand things compared to other people? Was it frustrating or embarrassing, or did you not mind?

Meaning: What did my delayed/mono-processing mean?

Did it take more mental effort and time for you to work out conversations or events? Did you misinterpret what people were saying or implying? Does mono-processing give you an advantage in spotting details or giving a perspective that no one else would ever see? How does your slower processing style affect your social interactions?

Effect: How did other people react?

Did people presume that you understood things immediately? When you seemed to be confused, did they offer you support to help you understand? Do you think people get impatient at your slower or unexpected responses? Did they believe you when you said you didn't understand something until later on?

Strategies: What strategies would support my delayed/mono-processing?

Would you find it useful to keep a journal to keep track of what is happening and develop a deeper awareness of when and why your processing might be delayed?

Can family and friends help by talking things through so everyone fully understands situations/conversations?

My spectrum of delayed/mono–processing

Record your thoughts and experiences here.

Event: What happened?

_____

_____

_____

_____

**Delayed reaction: What happened in my body
and mind after the event/conversation?**

_____

_____

_____

_____

Meaning: What did my delayed/mono—processing mean?

_____

_____

_____

_____

Effect: How did other people react?

_____

_____

_____

_____

**Strategies: What strategies would support
my delayed/mono—processing?**

_____

_____

_____

_____

This section outlines Finn's experiences of generalisation. You can use this to work out how you are affected when trying to generalise from one experience to another.

Finn's spectrum of generalisation

Event: What happened?

- *Finn was starting a new job and found it hard to know how to use her previous training to actually carry out the tasks.*

Repeat: What happened the next time Finn had to repeat this task/conversation?

- *Unable to remember and use the previously learnt information as it was only presented verbally and she can't take it all in at once or recall it unless it is written down.*

- *Gets stuck easily, especially with slight changes that totally baffle her. She can't work out what would be appropriate to do or how to adjust her actions to cope with new changes.*

- *Stood motionless trying to work out what to do as it was a different person and she did not know how to deal with this particular person's style of speaking and questions.*

- *Can't keep up with other people who seem to know everything with no apparent effort at all, so she has to copy them.*

- *Not realising that she needs help and/or thinking she can't ask for help as she is supposed to know what to do by now, like everyone else.*

Meaning: What did being unable to generalise mean for Finn?

- *Loss of confidence in her ability to do any job.*

- *Felt like giving up.*

- *Frustrated at being so slow and never knowing what to say or do even when she has done it before.*

- *Annoyed that it is so hard to use what she has been taught and apply it to real life.*

- *Embarrassed that she struggles so much to do simple things that others don't even have to think about.*

- *Her relentless determination keeps her mind focused on what needs to be done, no matter how many times she has to start again. Rigid, single-minded, goal-orientated thinking can be very useful indeed.*

Effect: How did other people react?

- *Gave her a second chance and let her observe someone else doing the job which gave her a mental template to copy from.*

- *Impatient annoyance at her incompetence, so they get someone else to take over.*

- *Slightly suspicious trying to figure her out, whether she's not trying hard enough or not paying attention or simply terribly lazy.*

- *Can't believe she took part in the training because she seems so clueless about what to do.*

Strategies: What would help Finn to generalise?

- *All possible different outcomes and ways of dealing with situations are verbally explained and given in written format to refer back to later on.*

- *The option to observe and audio record someone else dealing with several different situations so she can deal with a wider range of potential circumstances.*

- *Practical trial runs and interactive experiences to develop her own mental templates to absorb and work from.*

- *Visual demonstrations (YouTube, apps).*

Finn's spectrum of generalisation

Read Finn's creative writing. Do you think Finn finds it hard to cope with trying to generalise her knowledge from one situation to another?

What happened?

My mind goes blank, I've totally lost the ability to do this job. All my training seems to mean nothing at all.

Finn's ability to generalise

*Despite my thorough training
It seems I have no idea
Of what I have to say or do
In this particular situation.
I've got no mental templates
To guide me through these tasks
Every time
Is the first time
In whatever I do.
It does not matter
How much I know.
How long I have learnt it.
How hard I try.
I go right back to the start
To figure it all out again step by step
Then put all these parts into one whole picture in my mind.
For the one hundredth time.
Until I get to
One hundred and one!*

Being unable to generalise

I can't take these instructions
Guidelines and rules
To make them join together
Into something I can use.
They remain as separate parts
As I stand motionless unable to start
Until someone explains it all again.
With one-to-one demonstrations
Of what to do for this particular task.
Then if something changes
the next time round
Even the tiniest little bit
All those previous experiences
Set fast in my head
Become unfamiliar once again
Then I guess once more...
I am right back to the start.
I may as well have never done this before.

Other people's reactions

Puzzlement
Followed by disappointment
Followed by a lack of confidence
Followed by a slight suspicion
Should you really be doing this?
Sometimes followed by a second chance.

Finn's strategies

Multi-sensory activities

- Visual images/charts/diagrams

- Kinaesthetic – practical hands-on experiences

- Demonstrations & observation

- Auditory recordings

- Written preparation – script/instructions

- Self-reflection

- Preparation

- Observation

ACTIVITY G. YOUR WRITING PROMPTS

My spectrum of generalisation

(I have done this before but I feel like a beginner again)

Use the following vocabulary prompts and questions to complete your worksheet and then write your own poems, thoughts, mini-stories or narrative for each topic below.

Word prompts

Generalisation: Frustrating, embarrassing, slow, stupid, tired, unfair, stressful, tiring, boring, repetitive, lost, confused, panicked, sweaty, nervous, reluctant, hide, retreat, anxiety, worried, expectations, failure, determined, positive, adaptability, flexibility, rigidity.

Event: What happened?

When were you unable to use previously learnt information to deal with a new situation or task? A common small talk conversation, a science experiment, a practical task, PE games?

Repeat: What happened the next time I had to repeat this task/conversation?

Did you find that your mind was unable to take information from previous experiences in order to respond/act as expected in a different situation? How did this affect the conversation/situation/activity?

Meaning: What did being unable to generalise mean for me?

How does it make you feel if you don't always know what to do when presented with activities that you are expected to be able to do based on previous experiences? Does it make life harder to cope with because you find slight changes hard to adjust to? Do you get nervous, embarrassed, confused or tense, or go blank, when presented with any kind of new situation?

Effect: How did other people react?

Do you think people realise that having trouble generalising our knowledge from one situation to another is part of autism? Have people given extra explanations and support when needed? Will they get irritated or impatient when they expect that you should know what to say or do?

Strategies: What would help me to generalise?

Do you think using multi-sensory demonstrations with written, visual and verbal instructions would help? Could a social story provide the necessary background information to build on previous knowledge for new situations? How do you learn best when studying?

Would using study techniques to record and break down the information into steps allow your brain to process what to do in this particular situation so when something changes it will be easier for you to identify what to do next time?

ACTIVITY H. MY WORKSHEET

My spectrum of generalisation

(I have done this before but I feel like a beginner again)

Record your thoughts and experiences here.

Event: What happened?

_____

_____

_____

_____

**Repeat: What happened the next time I had
to repeat this task/conversation?**

_____

_____

_____

_____

Meaning: What did being unable to generalise mean for me?

_____

_____

_____

_____

_____

Effect: How did other people react?

_____

_____

_____

_____

_____

Strategies: What would help me to generalise?

_____

_____

_____

_____

_____

This section summarises Finn's experiences of processing differences. Read through it and use all the information that you have learnt about your processing differences to create your own profile.

What's Finn's spectrum of processing differences?

Finn's central coherence style means that she:

- *is able to see every aspect of a situation in more detail than most people*

- *can have a much deeper understanding of situations than other people because she can see all the individual parts in great detail*

- *knows how to put lots of small pieces together to create a different perspective*

- *requires extra time and explanations to understand topics/ situation/tasks*

- *has difficulty seeing the whole picture to automatically know what to do or how to keep talking*

- *needs to be given plenty of examples, instructions and opportunities to observe to let her copy until she can do things without having to work it all out*

- *finds it hard to retain all the separate bits of information in her mind at the same time.*

Finn's processing shutdowns mean that she:

- *reaches a state of processing exhaustion much quicker than other people and shuts down*

- *is unable to keep up with other people's level of social processing and gets very irritable*

- cannot process information properly once overwhelmed by activities, demands, socialising
- loses the ability to speak or think. Begins to operate on autopilot
- experiences this quite a lot for all sorts of reasons – tiredness, hunger, stress, doing too much, too many people, talking for too long, sensory overwhelm...

Finn's delayed/mono-processing means that she:

- has to think each stage through in parts to understand things
- sees everything one bit at a time, meaning her understanding may be limited
- takes longer to understand what conversations/questions mean
- never knows what to say or do at the right time
- gets left behind in conversations and then it's too late to give the appropriate response
- needs a lot more energy to take part in social events, which leaves her very tired
- can be judged as being rude, uncaring, cold, stupid.

Finn's generalisation style means that she:

- needs extra time to process tasks, demands and conversations to help her overcome generalising issues
- must learn all the separate parts for one task so she can deal with it independently
- will get stuck when presented with any slight changes as she cannot adapt her knowledge to something new
- might forget how to do something that she has done before, especially if something is different or she is stressed
- experiences a lot of stress and finds everything hard to cope with even if it is a straightforward-enough task.

Finn would like other people to:

- give her extra time, explanations and practical demonstrations to help her work out what to do

- check that she understood what they meant; check that they understand what she meant

- be patient and accept her different experiences of processing information as being real

- allow her to observe and copy, see, hear and do tasks for total comprehension. Then repeat this process

- understand she has a very different way of experiencing the world, making everything more complicated than they realise

- know that processing differences have a big effect on her experiences all the time.

ACTIVITY I. MY WORKSHEET

What's my spectrum of processing differences?

Record your thoughts and experiences here.

My central coherence style means that I:

_____

_____

_____

_____

My processing shutdowns mean that I:

_____

_____

_____

_____

My delayed/mono—processing means that I:

_____

_____

_____

_____

My generalisation style means that I:

_____

_____

_____

_____

I would like other people to:

_____

_____

_____

_____

What's Finn's spectrum of processing differences?

Read through Finn's creative writing and think about any similarities or differences that you have with Finn's profile of processing differences.

Finn's central coherence style

Observation strategies
Give me a chance to watch
And find a way to make myself
Fit into someone else's persona.
With this tactic I can work out what to say and how to act
It takes away the pressure of trying to figure it all out from scratch.
I can put all the separate pieces in my mind
Into one whole image to guide me through.
Copy and adapt is the easiest way for me to cope.

Finn's processing shutdowns

Too much is happening
For far too long.
Swallowed up by noises
Surrounded by people
System shutdown.
I can do no more.
Autopilot functioning switches on.

Finn's delayed/mono-processing

I see what is happening
It appears that I've got it.
But my mind stays blank.
What, how and why processed
As a sequence of separate events.
To be dissected apart
With a little more time
After the fact.

Or maybe never at all.
Only then can I have the chance to
Understand the point.
Absorb the possibilities.
Feel the consequences.

Finn's generalisation

I have no idea what to do
No matter how many times you saw me do it before
One situation is not the same as the next
I really mean it when I say
I have no idea what to say or do!!
Give me a chance to go back to the start
To be a beginner again and again and...

Dear people

Listen to me for a second or two
This brain of mine works remarkably differently it's true.
I'm very proud of all the things that I can do
The details I spot and how hard I am willing to work.
Sometimes though it can be frustrating too
As I have to make a huge effort just to keep up...really, truly quite a lot.
I think it's best if we find some kind of mutual understanding
Of all these additional factors no one ever thinks about.
Processing differences can have a big impact
Please keep them in mind and give consideration.
It's hard to always have to work things out.

What's my spectrum of processing differences?

Record your poems, thoughts and mini-stories here.

Why don't you write a poem or a story about:

- your style of processing

- anything that you would like to understand better

- what you would like other people to know about your spectrum of processing differences?

_____

_____

_____

_____

_____

_____

_____

_____

_____

_____

ACTIVITY K. MY PROFILE CHART

My processing differences profile

Strengths	Challenges
•	•
•	•
•	•
•	•
•	•

Goals

•

•

•

•

•

Strategies

•

•

•

•

•

Top three things you need to know about me

•

•

•

Chapter 4

Know Your Spectrum of Theory of Mind

Introduction

Jokes, sarcasm and hidden meanings

The term theory of mind describes our ability to understand that other people have different thoughts and feelings to us. It allows us to interpret social interactions and predict what other people might say or do. With autism we can have a different way of processing and using verbal language and body language. We might miss body language cues and not understand facial expressions or be able to identify which social cues we need to pay attention to. When someone is speaking and they change their tone of voice or emphasise certain words, we might not notice or understand what these variations in tone mean and imply. People use these changes to show when they are joking, being sarcastic or what they are really feeling inside. Their words may not match what they really mean or feel, but we might not realise this, meaning we miss the point of a comment or joke, which could lead to miscommunications or conversations stalling. These differences in how we communicate and interpret verbal interactions mean that there can be a lot of confusion! Other people may not understand that we do not have the same way of communicating, and this can lead to misunderstandings.

We tend to speak in a very honest and straightforward way which can sometimes seem very blunt. We mean exactly what we say and don't have any hidden meanings behind our words. Other people can presume we are implying stuff, as that is what usually happens in conversations, but we haven't thought beyond exactly what we are saying. We also believe that what people say is exactly what they mean. We trust what we are told and don't look for motives or the hidden meaning behind words.

Understanding other people's thoughts

We might not realise that other people have thoughts, opinions or emotions that are different to our own, which means we can have problems anticipating what other people will say or do (Edelson 2017). Or if we do understand that other people are thinking or feeling something different to us we might find it difficult to figure out what that might be (Soraya 2018). Our responses or actions might be based on what we are thinking, rather than reacting to the other person's needs or desires. This can make us seem insensitive as we might say or do things that are not what would be expected. However, this is just how our minds automatically work. We are responding in a way that is logical for us but may not be understood by others.

We tend to speak from a factual perspective and use logic to work out what to say rather than trying to respond to the other person's hidden meaning or the emotions behind their words. Sometimes because we are thinking of situations or people in a logical way we can say too much and not realise that we might hurt someone by being too honest and blunt. If someone asks us a question we will give them an honest answer, whereas other people tend to tell 'white lies' to avoid being too truthful and possibly hurting someone's feelings. Then we may not know that we have said something wrong or pick up the signs that the other person is annoyed or wants to talk about something else.

It may be that we are unable to identify what it is that we don't understand about a conversation to allow us to ask for things to be explained and sort out any misunderstandings. If someone asks us a question we may find it hard to know what to tell them and what to leave out (Attwood 2008). We may also experience delayed processing which will further affect our comprehension of interactions. All this stuff has to be worked out logically and usually later on when we have had time to think it through, but it might be too late at this stage to correct any mix-ups.

Literalism

When people speak we take their words literally, so when they say 'It is raining cats and dogs', our automatic understanding will be that cats and dogs are raining down from the sky instead of referring to the large volume of rainfall. As we tend to be visual thinkers we might automatically get an image in our brain that literally represents what someone said. Common sayings, such as metaphors, can be tricky for us to understand and we tend to take them literally, so 'He is a walking dictionary' means that we see a dictionary walking along the street and wonder how someone can be a walking dictionary (i.e. they know a lot!).

If we are asked 'can' we do something, our minds may not register that there is an implication behind the question for us to actually do a task. We take the words literally to mean are we actually capable of doing this job rather than 'Do it!'

This way of thinking and interpreting language can cause us to misunderstand lots of conversations and it might confuse other people too. Having to work out so many things can make us feel very anxious and self-conscious of others noticing if we make a mistake or that we are different. We might constantly feel like we are living on a different planet to everyone else and they all know what to say or do while we are struggling to keep up.

Our different way of thinking also means that we can be very naive and trusting of other people. If we don't use or pick up on hidden meanings or implications, or appreciate the fact that people think differently to us, then these differences might be obvious to someone else. They might realise that we are very literal and believe every word they say without questioning if they have ulterior motives. This means a certain type of person might use these differences to manipulate us in some way. They might make fun of us and we won't actually know this is what they are doing, which could make us vulnerable, especially when combined with our processing differences and rigid thinking style.

Asking for help

When we are having problems we don't always realise that someone else can help us and we might keep our difficulties to ourselves (Attwood 2008). Even when we do understand that a particular person can help us, it still may not occur to us to actually speak up and ask for help. We might just continue with what we are doing regardless of how much we need help. Our minds tend to be a bit inflexible so we can't identify all the options (Attwood 2008). This could have a big effect on us if we don't get the necessary help at the right time.

Our theory of mind is individual to us; some autistic people might find the language differences really hard to understand, while others might have no problem in getting jokes and being sarcastic, though this will likely have been learnt over time. All these various skills that relate to our theory of mind tend to be delayed and have to be worked out. As we get older and more experienced we become more able to understand these language differences (Attwood 2007).

The influence of theory of mind is important in our daily lives as it allows us to work out what is going on around us. If we find out how theory of mind affects us we can start to understand how we think and process language. By doing this, we might gradually learn to spot when we are experiencing confusion with our interpretation of interactions and learn when and how to get help when we need it. It will also allow us to identify other people who don't have good intentions. This should then help to prevent any misunderstandings or difficulties we are experiencing from escalating into a bigger problem and allow us to be supported when we need it.

This section outlines Finn's tendency to miss jokes, sarcasm or hidden meanings. You can use it to work out your own spectrum of missing jokes, sarcasm or hidden meanings.

Finn's spectrum of missing the joke, sarcasm or hidden meaning

What happens when Finn does not understand?

- **Jokes:** Has to work out what the punch line meant. She may laugh but not really have a clue what was funny. Though she is much better at getting jokes now.

- **Sarcasm:** Will not always understand the implications behind words or the change in tone to show when someone is being sarcastic. People say one thing but they are really having a joke, mocking or putting her or someone else down.

- **Hidden meanings:** Understands that people can have hidden meanings but usually cannot identify them unless they get annoyed. Then they accuse her of knowing exactly what they meant!

Event: When does Finn miss the joke, sarcasm or hidden meaning?

- In fast conversations or groups with lots of people talking as she has to be able to remember what was said and then work out the meaning of the words spoken too.

- Takes thing literally so won't always understand the language used, even if she picks up on what the other person's tone of voice is suggesting.

- Never thinks of hidden meanings as she does not do this in conversations.

- If she does not know someone very well and has not figured out how the other person thinks or their humour.

- When someone else realises she will not understand jokes, sarcasm or hidden intentions and tries to trick her or make fun of her on purpose.

Meaning: What does this mean for Finn?

- She can be unintentionally funny when she confuses jokes.

- People presume she has gotten the point and might not believe her confusion or lack of reaction.

- Can feel left out if she is the only one who doesn't get the joke and has to pretend to understand.

- May be laughed at or cause other people to get irritated without understanding why.

Strategies: What can Finn do to understand the joke, sarcasm and hidden meaning?

- Discuss what was said with someone who understands her confusion and can help her work out what was meant.

- Create a cartoon story to help her process conversations and the different types of speech.

Finn's spectrum of missing the joke, sarcasm or hidden meaning

Read Finn's creative writing. How do you think having a different way of understanding language would affect Finn's social interactions with other people?

What happens when Finn does not understand?

Jokes can be a mystery. I've no idea what's so funny. Play pretend, laugh along, no one ever really knows how much I don't understand.

Sarcasm, I sometimes get it with someone who I know very well. But with someone new I can never be quite sure if they are being serious or if they mean the opposite of what they said. I can't quite pinpoint what the tone of their voice means nor do I understand the meaning of their words.

As for hidden meaning, not for one second do I think they meant anything more than what they actually said...because I mean what I say, every time, with no hints of any kind.

When Finn misses the joke, sarcasm or hidden meaning

It seems I am the only one who doesn't get the funny side as I laugh with all my body while quietly wondering 'What was so funny?' Sometimes it makes me feel like I am an outsider. But then again it can be quite amusing when I misinterpret sarcastic hints, making those around me laugh, which creates a sort of warmth that stretches across the differences between us both.

Meaning for Finn

No idea that I missed the hidden meaning so I simply carry on. But these conversation time bombs tick, tick, tick...10 hours later I realise what was meant.

Why am I always the last to know?
How can I be so slow?

Then I feel ever so tense. I am wrecked with anxious thoughts. They churn all around, filling me with a paranoid confusion. Then suddenly I realise, they were making fun of me, while pretending to be my friend.

Finn's strategies

Post-conversation analysis helps me understand what is happening. Helps me to spot those who choose to mock or trick. Though it's usually far too late. Maybe with help from another trusted person, a storyboard to visualise the situation, it may become apparent what the subtle cues of the conversation actually were.

ACTIVITY A. YOUR WRITING PROMPTS

My spectrum of missing the joke, sarcasm or hidden meaning

Use the following vocabulary prompts and questions to complete your worksheet and then write your own poems, thoughts, mini-stories or narrative for each topic below.

Word prompts

Jokes, sarcasm, hidden meaning: Laughter, confusion, lost, slow, funny, amusing, humorous, entertaining, comical, droll, witty, sarcastic, ironic, mocking, sardonic, scornful, tone, pitch, suggestive, disdainful, derisive, satirical, cutting, sharp, hurtful, concealed, secret, concrete thinking, logical, straight-forward, delayed thinking, trusting, gullible, naive, susceptible, single-track mind.

What happens when I do not understand?

Do you find conversations hard to follow due to misinterpretations of language? Are you often left feeling confused during or after conversations?

When you don't understand a joke, sarcasm or hidden meaning, what usually happens? Does it create deeper connections, arguments or laughter?

Event: When do I miss the joke, sarcasm or hidden meaning?

Do you have to work out why people find something funny or if they are being sarcastic or implying something? Does this happen a lot or can you usually get what people mean most of the time? Is your understanding often delayed or literal?

Do you usually notice any changes of tone in people's voices? Are there particular occasions or people that this seems to happen more with? Why do you think this is? Does the topic or the speed of a conversation make it more difficult to pick up on underlying meanings or tone of voice?

Meaning: What does this mean for me?

How does your different use and understanding of language make you feel? Do you get annoyed and feel stupid or do you find it funny? Does it make you feel different or left out?

How do other people react towards your responses? Are they mistrustful and suspicious of you or do they find it funny and explain things to you? What do you think could happen if you don't get a hidden meaning in a conversation?

Strategies: What can I do to understand the joke, sarcasm and hidden meaning?

Would it help to use social stories with explanations of what was said to understand what was meant? Do you feel able to ask people directly for further support in working these things out?

Could you learn to understand particular aspects of language through a script or by watching a TV show with examples of sarcasm/hidden meanings included? If you kept a record of common sayings, could this develop your awareness of the implied meaning?

My spectrum of missing the joke, sarcasm or hidden meaning

Record your thoughts and experiences here.

What happens when I do not understand?

Jokes:

_____

_____

_____

_____

Sarcasm:

_____

_____

_____

_____

Hidden meaning:

_____

_____

_____

Event: When do I miss the joke, sarcasm or hidden meaning?

_____

_____

_____

_____

_____

Meaning: What does this mean for me?

_____

_____

_____

_____

_____

Strategies: What can I do to understand the joke, sarcasm and hidden meaning?

_____

_____

_____

_____

_____

This section outlines Finn's experiences with understanding what people are thinking. It will allow you to identify your experience of understanding other people's thoughts.

Finn's spectrum of understanding other people's thoughts

Reasons: Why might Finn not understand other people's thoughts?

- *Does not occur to her that other people will think something different as she has everything worked out.*

- *Rigid thinking style means that she may not see all the possible perspectives in a situation until someone else gives an opinion which can be a surprise to her!*

- *Processing delays will mean her comprehension of events will occur after everything is over.*

- *Limited attempts to communicate will result in less awareness of the possible perspectives.*

- *Difficulty predicting what people will say or do next.*

Effect: How do other people react?

- *Most of the time Finn doesn't say anything and keeps her surprise to herself, so other people presume the understanding is mutual.*

- *Annoyed at something she has said as it is totally unexpected and possibly inappropriate.*

- *With mistrust; they think that her perspective is simply a way to start an argument or to annoy them on purpose.*

- *People ask a question and when they get a response they are annoyed as they didn't really want it answered honestly or with so much detail and logic.*

Meaning: What might this mean for Finn?

- *Surprised to learn someone else thought something different and she had not even considered it.*

- *Shocked that other people have different and hidden intentions that motivate their actions or words which are not always good.*

- *Perplexed to find out that someone is annoyed about her response when she was only answering the question they asked.*

- *Will not occur to her that other people might have bad intentions which could make her vulnerable to those who realise her naivety.*

Strategies: How can Finn deal with this?

- *Avoid long paragraphs explaining things in great detail that make perfectly logical sense to her as it is often not appreciated!*

- *Keep her thoughts to herself as long as she understands things, then just let other people think differently.*

- *Share her thoughts through a poem as it is a direct way of communicating, which will make it easier for someone else to relate to the emotions behind the situation.*

- *Reflect on events to understand other people and their motives to make sure it is safe to be with them.*

Finn's spectrum of understanding other people's thoughts

Read Finn's creative writing. What do you think Finn would find most difficult about having trouble understanding other people's thoughts?

Other people's thoughts

I've got my opinion
Got it all worked out
Usually three hours behind
With one fact at a time.
But not for one second
Does it occur to me to speak
'Why would they think anything differently to me?'
You see other people's thoughts
Are quite a surprise
They come from nowhere
Completely unexpectedly.
Leaving me quietly wondering
In my silent retreat
'Whatever will they say next?'

Other people's reactions

Most of the time
They don't actually know
As I said before...
Not for one second
Does it occur to me to speak!

Meaning for Finn

Keeping quiet
Lessens misunderstandings
Increases confusion
Then when I suddenly decide to respond
It all goes ever so wrong!!

Finn's strategies

Don't answer questions
No matter who asks.
Don't write it down
To get every point across.
Don't speak
Don't write
Shut up!

Maybe a poem...

Shh!!

ACTIVITY C. YOUR WRITING PROMPTS

My spectrum of understanding other people's thoughts

Use the following vocabulary prompts and questions to complete your worksheet and then write your own poems, thoughts, mini-stories or narrative for each topic below.

Word prompts

Perspectives: Perceptions, viewpoints, feelings, observations, insights, understanding, standpoints, intuition, surprise, disbelief, unexpected, shock, confusion, puzzled, honest, misunderstanding, misperception, anxiety, disagreements, differences, assumed, believed, implicit, expected, supposed, presumed, trusting, naive, tricked, manipulation, vulnerable, risk, gullible, inflexible, narrow perspective, delayed processing.

Reasons: Why might I not understand other people's thoughts?

Do you have a rigid black and white style of thinking that means you might only see certain aspects of a situation? Are you able to predict what people might say or do by previous experiences with them? Do you prefer to say exactly what you think rather than tell 'white lies'?

Is your processing of information delayed so it takes longer to work things out? Does confusion over how language is used make it harder to understand what people are thinking?

Effect: How do other people react?

What do people think of your ability to understand their perspective? Is there a lot of confusion or arguments about people's different opinions on things?

Are people annoyed as they think you understand and use language the way they do? Do they think you are too honest?

Meaning: What might this mean for me?

Are people's words and actions unexpected? How do you feel when you realise you have a different interpretation or don't understand an interaction? Do you end up having disagreements or confusion about what you meant and what others intended?

Is it confusing to find that no one else seems to think like you? Do you say exactly what you think with total honesty and then other people don't react well?

Do you trust people's words without thinking about why they are saying something? What could this lead to if you never understood another person's thoughts?

Strategies: How can I deal with this?

Would writing out situations or creating a spidergram be a useful way of identifying all the different opinions/perspectives to understand each person's feelings and what is going on?

Could family and friends support you in working out how to deal with any situations that are confusing?

My spectrum of understanding other people's thoughts

Record your thoughts and experiences here.

Reasons: Why might I not understand other people's thoughts?

_____

_____

_____

Effect: How do other people react?

_____

_____

_____

Meaning: What might this mean for me?

_____

_____

_____

Strategies: How can I deal with this?

_____

_____

_____

This section outlines Finn's spectrum of taking words literally. It will help you identify your own way of understanding and using language literally.

Finn's spectrum of taking words literally

Event: When Finn took words literally:

- 'You're like a robot.'
  Meaning: You are not showing much emotion.
  Finn's reaction: Instant image flashes up in her head – metal arms, legs, body, square head, clasp tight in 30 seconds flat.

- 'Did the cat get your tongue?'
  Meaning: You are not speaking very much.
  Finn's reaction: Open mouth, eyes straight down, tongue wiggle, frown... 'A cat??'

- A child running towards the sea shouts 'Waves!!'
  Meaning: Look at the sea waves.
  Finn's reaction: Finn waved her hands in response to their request...

- 'He had a heart of gold.'
  Meaning: He was a good person.
  Finn's reaction: Looks straight at his heart while wondering to herself 'Is that not too heavy to carry around?'

Meaning: What does literal thinking mean for Finn?

- Literalism is her automatic way of thinking. A lot of confusion and misunderstandings can occur without being able to identify why.

- Arguments about what was meant or not, resulting in distrust, 'She must have understood.'

- Takes other people's words and interprets them as meaning exactly what they said, so people's statements mean one thing and one thing only, then her sometimes rigid black and white thinking style further reduces her ability to see what was meant.

- *If she takes words literally then this can lead to hyper-sensitivity about others' negative comments as she believes exactly what they say.*

- *Does not question what people mean. Bases her understanding on precise, factual interpretations.*

- *Naively trusting of people's words, which could make her a target for those who want to make fun of her or confuse her on purpose.*

Effect: When Finn uses words literally and means exactly what she says:

- *Can cause great confusion, as she has one understanding which is very different to what the person speaking intended.*

- *Other people make up their own interpretations despite her speaking the exact words that she means.*

- *People think she is being silly or rude on purpose or unbelievably slow.*

- *Distrust that she does not really mean something else as hidden implications exist behind most people's words.*

- *She will see images in her mind that are exactly what people said which can be really quite ridiculous.*

Strategies: How can Finn deal with literal thinking?

- *Explain that she has a literal way of thinking so other people can help her to understand.*

- *Ask people to speak in a way that will help her know what they mean.*

- *Question everything that people say – work out what they meant before accepting the words they use.*

Finn's spectrum of taking words literally

Read Finn's creative writing. What do you think might happen when Finn uses and understands language literally? Why do you think the adjudicator asked her if she had cold feet?

Finn's literal understanding

I stood frozen at the edge of the stage but not one word would come out. When it was over the adjudicator asked **'Did you get cold feet?'** Well I stood and stared back quite blankly. **'Not at all'**, I thought to myself, **'I have lovely warm socks on.'** Then I puzzled over what possible reason he would want to know about my feet and walked off, leaving him waiting for a response.

Finn's literal thinking

Confusion can become a regular way of life with words and sayings that I just can't help but hear exactly as they are. So my eyes look around for that tasty **'Piece of cake'** until I realise there really is no cake...then I wonder **'How can a cake be easy?'** Though it's funny all the same as this literal sort of brain flashes up some really peculiar pictures in my mind. At the same time misunderstandings about someone else's words can lead to arguments over things that were only a passing comment. Even worse, sometimes it can be used against me as a way of making me feel stupid, which is a pretty unpleasant thing to do.

Finn means exactly what she says

I mean exactly what I say
Literally
Factually
Actually
Accurately
Correctly
No other meaning intended.

Get it?

NO THEY DON'T!!!!

Finn's strategies

Think
Talk
Analyse
Question

Be aware of my literal thinking
All this will help to avoid confusion!!

ACTIVITY E. YOUR WRITING PROMPTS

My spectrum of taking words literally

Use the following vocabulary prompts and questions to complete your worksheet and then write your own poems, thoughts, mini-stories or narrative for each topic below.

Word prompts

Literalism: Believe what people say, take words exactly as they are spoken, visual images of exactly what people say, concrete thinking, gullible, naive, trusting, easy to fool, susceptible, innocent, incredulous, actual, precise, logical, straightforward, to the point, direct, confused, accept as true, unquestioning, black and white thinking, arguments, misunderstandings, implications, suggestions, sensitive, blunt.

Event: When I took words literally:

When people speak literally, what happens in your mind both during and after the interaction? Do other people seem rude when they use sayings like 'Break a leg?'

Do you take verbal instructions literally and then do something that isn't expected?

Meaning: What does literal thinking mean for me?

Does it cause laughter, embarrassments, arguments or misunderstandings? Does literalism lead to funny incidents? Do you not always understand the underlying implications to say or do things?

Are you usually the last person to understand things? How does that make you feel?

Effect: When I use words literally and mean exactly what I say:

Are you able to identify when you have taken words literally and need things explained? Do you find that how you use and understand language is different to other people? Are you very precise when describing things and then expect other people to be the same?

How does literalism affect your relationships? Are you considered to be very honest and straight to the point?

Strategies: How can I deal with literal thinking?

Would it help to make a visual record or cartoon strip using metaphors and examples of literal thinking to show the images they create in your mind to help others understand how your brain thinks?

What would be most helpful in allowing you to understand language – verbal explanations, role plays, discussions, writing it down, drawing, checking definitions online?

My spectrum of taking words literally

Record your thoughts and experiences here.

Event: When I took words literally:

_____

_____

_____

Meaning: What does literal thinking mean for me?

_____

_____

_____

Effect: When I use words literally and mean exactly what I say:

_____

_____

_____

Strategies: How can I deal with literal thinking?

_____

_____

_____

This section outlines Finn's experiences of forgetting or not being able to ask for help. You can use this as an example to write about your experiences of getting help.

Finn's spectrum of forgetting or feeling unable to ask for help

Events: When did Finn forget or feel unable to ask for help?

- *In a classroom when stuck on a problem and she doesn't think to actually tell someone that she needs help.*

- *Too busy trying to remember the instructions to be able to stop, think and ask for help.*

- *Playing PE games and she can't remember the rules and the teacher said that everyone knows exactly what to do so there is no need for a word to be spoken. So she takes this statement literally and will not speak one word even to get help.*

- *At a party and she feels uncomfortable with the people she is with but they all seem to be having fun.*

- *In a group with too many people, there is no chance that she will speak.*

Reasons: What might make Finn forget or feel unable to ask for help?

- *A rigid style of thinking means it does not even occur to her that there are different options including asking for help or that getting help is a possibility.*

- *Her mind will think in a straight line and miss all the signals that show when, who or how to ask for help.*

- *Hyper-focus on what she is doing so her brain does not see anything else and the next stage of taking action to get help is not obvious.*

- *Temporary shutdowns or meltdowns will mean she is unable to think or speak properly.*

- *If she has done it before and then something has changed, it may not occur to Finn that she can still ask for help, because she thinks she is expected to know from previous experience.*

- *If in a group and everyone else knows what to do she might be too embarrassed to ask out loud and have all that attention on her.*

- *Communication difficulties mean that even if she realises she needs help she will not say one word, especially if in a group situation.*

Meaning: What does this mean for Finn?

- *Might feel unable to do things if she keeps getting stuck and can't get help.*

- *Frustration when she is unable to do something and realises too late that she could have asked for help.*

- *Can seem to not need any support because she never asks for help or shows any visible reactions to being stuck.*

- *Could be vulnerable if she is in trouble, unsure or uncomfortable and she forgets or it does not occur to her that she can ask for help.*

- *Other people may not register she needs help especially as she rarely shows any signs of distress.*

Strategies: What can Finn do to make sure she can get help?

- *A set of questions to be asked during any task. Then without needing to realise whether she needs help she will automatically find out by following her prepared system every time.*

- *Set a timer at intervals to make her stop and ask questions to check and work out if she needs help.*

- *Make sure other people know that the possibility to ask for help might not occur to her so they can check that she is alright.*

Finn's spectrum of forgetting or feeling unable to ask for help

Read Finn's creative writing. Do you think Finn's difficulties asking for help would have a significant impact on her?

What happened?

I sat with my head stuck down trying to finish my work in maths class. Totally lost as to how to do this very complicated word problem even though I had done this type of sum before. It was only when it was much too late that it clicked in my one-track, straight-thinking kind of mind...**"Why didn't I ask anyone for help?"** But then again, it didn't really matter as I wouldn't have ever opened my mouth to speak in a crowd or let them see how much I didn't know when we did this topic only last week. While all these thoughts go through my mind, not a flicker of distress will appear on my face. I never, ever ask for help! I often don't even think of it!

Reasons Finn might forget or feel unable to ask for help

When I should know what to do
How do I say?
I haven't got a clue?

Hyper-focus
Meltdowns
Super-fast shutdowns
Not for one second does the possibility occur to shout
Help!!

Asking for help
Takes a flexible kind of mind.
Able to see the possibilities all around.

Meaning for Finn

Maths is a pain
I'd rather be stuck out in the rain.
What am I supposed to do?
When I don't have the slightest clue
Or even think to say one word that might get me some help!
I think I'll just give up!!

Finn's strategies to get help

3Qs

- *What is happening?*
- *Do I know what to do?*
- *Who can help me?*

ACTIVITY G. YOUR WRITING PROMPTS

My spectrum of forgetting or feeling unable to ask for help

Use the following vocabulary prompts and questions to complete your worksheet and then write your own poems, thoughts, mini-stories or narrative for each topic below.

Word prompts

Help: Assistance, aid, support, assist, stuck, caught, focused mind, rigid thoughts, options, alternatives, forget, disregard, overlook, not recall, realisation, worried, overwhelmed, circular thoughts, reduced options, possibilities, bear in mind, narrow thinking, afraid, self-conscious, embarrassed, unsure.

Event: When did I forget or feel unable to ask for help?

Think of a time when you needed help. Were you able to ask for help when you needed it?

Are you afraid of appearing to be stupid in front of your class?

Reasons: What might make me forget or feel unable to ask for help?

Do you have trouble working out who to turn to for help? Do shutdowns or meltdowns affect your ability to ask for help or see the available options? Will delayed processing mean you don't realise you need or could ask for help?

If you are supposed to know what to do because you have done it before, will you feel unable to ask for support?

Meaning: What does this mean for me?

Do you miss opportunities to get support? Does this mean you might give up on completing things?

How do you feel when you can't ask for help or don't know what to do? Will you keep working at something even when it is not going well rather than try another tactic or get help?

Strategies: What can I do to make sure I can get help?

Do you think a written plan outlining what you need to do would allow you to see when you are stuck? Would it be useful to have deadlines to meet so that if you don't meet them you can start to question if you need to ask for help?

Could family or friends help you to identify areas you might need support with? If you are in class could you arrange a personal signal or code word with your teacher that shows you need help or aren't sure?

My spectrum of forgetting or feeling unable to ask for help

Record your thoughts and experiences here.

Event: When did I forget or feel unable to ask for help?

_____

_____

_____

_____

Reasons: What might make me forget or feel unable to ask for help?

_____

_____

_____

_____

Meaning: What does this mean for me?

_____

_____

_____

_____

_____

Strategies: What can I do to make sure I can get help?

_____

_____

_____

_____

_____

This section provides a summary of Finn's spectrum of theory of mind. Read through it and use all the information you have learnt about yourself throughout this chapter to create your own version.

What's Finn's spectrum of theory of mind?

Finn can find it hard to understand social interactions when she:

- doesn't always get the joke, sarcasm or hint

- misses the hidden meanings of conversations

- is surprised that other people have different thoughts or opinions to her

- speaks literally and thinks literally but other people presume there are hidden meanings

- takes people's words literally and believes everything she is told without question

- naively trusts other people's use of language and intentions which could be risky for her.

To be able to understand everything that is happening around her Finn needs to:

- understand how she uses and understands language, then share this information with other people

- have jokes, hints, sarcasm and implications explained to her if needed

- learn to recognise how much to say and when to say nothing

- be spoken to without double meanings. Not have double meanings added to her words

- be aware that other people's motivations or thoughts might be different to how she thinks

- understand that compared to other people she is naive and trusting

- learn to question everything and identify when someone may not be honest or have good intentions.

Finn can ask for help when needed by:

- remembering that she will not always know when she needs help and to have a checking system to keep track of when she might need help

- identifying who would be able to help her for different types of problems

- working out what to say or do to get help before something happens

- having someone who is aware of her difficulties and who can help her identify when she needs help

- being aware that, in any situation or with any person, help can be asked for and given even if she has done this task before.

Finn would like other people to:

- understand that this is an area that she often has a lot of confusion with

- say exactly what they mean

- explain what they mean if she does not understand

- understand that she means what she says – which can seem very blunt

- give her extra time to process their words and actions

- be aware that she may need help and not realise it

- understand that when she is stuck she may not know how to actually get help

- know that she may be unable to communicate the words to ask for help

- realise that she may look absolutely fine no matter how much help is needed.

ACTIVITY I. MY WORKSHEET

What's my spectrum of theory of mind?

Record your thoughts and experiences here.

I can find it hard to understand social interactions when I:

_____

_____

_____

To be able to understand everything that is happening around me I need to:

_____

_____

_____

I can ask for help when needed by:

_____

_____

_____

I would like other people to:

_____

_____

_____

What's Finn's spectrum of theory of mind?

Read Finn's creative writing. Consider what similarities or differences you have with Finn's experiences of theory of mind.

Theory of mind is...

Double meanings
Jokes and jibes
Sarcastic comments
Hints and lies
I've no comprehension of all these social ties.
I mean what I say
Then work out your words long after they have been spoken.
Do you really have to make everything so complicated??
I don't seem to be thinking the same thing as anyone else
Sometimes it's funny
Other times this makes me feel a little bit lonely
Especially when someone seems to have made me feel bad intentionally
With my unquestioningly naive trust in their words.
Made even worse when I don't even think to ask for help!
I have to conclude
It's all a little bit confusing
I think I'll stick to my straightforward way of thinking
It's so much easier to understand everything that's inside my own head!

ACTIVITY J. MY WORKSHEET

What's my spectrum of theory of mind?

Record your poems, thoughts or mini-stories here.

Why don't you write a poem or a story about:

- your experiences related to how you experience theory of mind

- any areas you would like to develop

- what you would like other people to know about your spectrum of theory of mind?

_____

_____

_____

_____

_____

_____

_____

_____

_____

ACTIVITY K. MY PROFILE CHART

My theory of mind profile

Strengths	Challenges
•	•
•	•
•	•
•	•
•	•

Strategies	Goals
•	•
•	•
•	•
•	•
•	•

Top three things you need to know about me

•

•

•

5

Know Your Spectrum of Social Communication

Introduction

Social communication difficulties

Social communication allows us to join in with social activities and helps us to make friends. Talking in social situations can be difficult for us, as we have to use our intellect to work out what to say and do. This means we have to think about what to say in each exchange rather than automatically know what would be good to talk about next. We may not have enough social imagination to help us think of what to talk about. Conversations have to be analysed and thought through in a logical way in order for us to absorb and work out what the other person is saying and then what we will say in response. This means there can be pauses when we are speaking, so our conversations might falter. Other people can participate in social interactions naturally, using their intuition. This means they don't have to think about what to say, they just know instinctively. While everyone else seems to find it easy to know what to say and to keep the conversation flowing, we may struggle to do the same.

As we learnt in the chapter on theory of mind we tend to be very honest and direct with our words and say exactly what we mean, though sometimes this can lead to our words being too blunt and possibly seeming rude. Most people don't say what they mean and their words will have hidden meanings which they will expect us to react to, but we don't pick up on the hints. People might also decide we really mean something else, which can lead to misjudgements. We might not be able to read other people's body language, know how close to stand to someone or use appropriate eye contact. All these theory of mind differences will influence our ability to socialise.

It can be hard for us to know how to start conversations, when to stop talking or we can go completely mute and can't say one word, making us feel very awkward. When we take part in conversations we might not find the right time to join in and our words don't seem to be heard. Or we might be very enthusiastic and end up saying too much and not pick up when to stop or take turns. This might lead other people to think we are interrupting and taking over conversations.

We might repeat sentences or words that we heard somewhere else as part of conversations (which is called echolalia). This might help us to socialise better or the words might seem out of place and so make conversations hesitate or stop altogether. Often we can be prepared to speak with a ready-made script, but the conversation does not go the way we expected and we end up left behind while everyone else carries on talking without any extra thought or effort required to take part.

Our different way of processing information may lead to us only understanding parts of conversations, or we may experience delayed processing, meaning we don't fully understand things until we have had time to think it through. Our ability to generalise our previous knowledge from one social situation to another will also influence how easily we can interact.

Speaking inconsistencies

Our ability to speak can change from day to day or even within minutes, so we might suddenly shut down and find that it is almost impossible to say one syllable, which can make us seem irritable and withdrawn. We can have good days when we are more able to speak well and connect, but the next day we switch right back to the beginning and can't speak very well. Sometimes we can become frozen and unable to function at all in a social interaction as we get into a state of extreme self-consciousness and can't relax to speak properly, so our words become hesitant and disjointed or we become temporarily mute. When we change so much, it can make people question our behaviour as it doesn't always match across circumstances or with different people. Our speaking ability seems to be inconsistent to those around us and they may not understand why as there is no apparent reason for it.

Making friends

As all these differences in our social communication are internal, they are invisible. Sometimes people feel we are not making an effort as it looks like we are not doing much on the surface, but, in reality, underneath we are working very hard to keep things in balance and speak well. People might think we are being unfriendly or rude and that we are doing it on purpose when we don't interact or speak as expected. Even when we work hard to try to fit in and chat with others, often we don't make the same connection and friendships don't develop. It can be very frustrating to keep trying and not have the same impact that someone without autism will have.

We also need to have a point to any activity we do, otherwise we lose motivation. Social activities that most people enjoy such as 'small talk' can seem pointless to us, which can mean we lose interest. These types of conversations are how other people develop bonds and get to know each other, leading to friendships. We just aren't motivated by social interactions in the way other people are, as we don't really get the same sense of connection that other people do through general everyday social chatting. Autistic people are more likely to connect through their common interests and discussing topics that are important to them.

Differences in how males and females present

There can also be differences between how males and females present in social situations. Females are often judged more on their social skills and there can be extra pressure to act like their peers. Autistic girls tend to 'mask', which means we hide our real responses and autistic behaviours to try to fit in. Girls might spend a lot of time watching and analysing other people to work out how they speak and interact, learning to mimic and adapt to different situations. Autistic girls are often described as chameleons and can fit in to such an extent that no one even realises they have any social difficulties at all, but they have to work very hard to keep up this mask of being the same as everyone else. They may still have trouble developing friendships and maintaining relationships.

Boys might be less interested in creating or hiding behind a persona during social interactions, so their autism might be more apparent. It just depends on the individual and how motivated they are to succeed socially.

Social burnout

Socialising can feel like a lot of hard work for us because we have to think about everything we are saying and doing. It can take a huge amount of effort and energy, leaving us feeling exhausted and unable to speak by the end of a social occasion or probably when we are halfway through it. We simply can't cope with the same volume of socialising as other people as it is so much effort for us. If we have too many social demands to meet, we might get to the stage that we experience social burnout and can no longer communicate or socialise for a while. Our bodies and minds shut down and stop functioning properly, and to overcome this, the best option is to withdraw. We have a genuine need to spend time on our own to recover from socialising because that is how our bodies and minds are able to feel good again.

Socialising and meeting people can create invisible barriers for us, and being with people may make us feel very nervous and uncomfortable or different. All these differences in our communication styles can also mean we can be misunderstood and misjudged. We might feel as if we never seem to get things quite right, despite putting a lot of effort into socialising. This can lead us to feeling bad about ourselves and maybe wanting to give up trying.

It might help us to find out who we are in social situations and how they affect us. Then we can learn to recognise what we can cope with and what causes us problems, and begin to think about how we can deal with social situations. This will allow us to decide how and when we want to socialise so that we can take part in social activities, but still feel good about ourselves and inside our bodies.

This section outlines Finn's social communication difficulties. It can be used as a template to identify your own spectrum of social communication difficulties.

Finn's spectrum of social communication difficulties

Event: What happened?

- *Finn tried to make conversation with other girls her age but was unable to keep the conversation flowing and it was a very awkward and uncomfortable situation.*

Reaction: What happened in Finn's body and mind?

Body	Mind
- *Tense, shaky, mute* - *Blushing* - *Feels sick, nervous* - *Hesitant eye contact/words*	- *No words available that will come out properly* - *Extreme self-consciousness* - *Embarrassed, feels like she's weird* - *Panic, can't think, wants to leave*

Delayed reaction: What happened in Finn's body and mind afterwards?

Body	Mind
- *Drained, legs feel like jelly* - *Tension and tears pour out* - *Irritable*	- *Feeling useless and annoyed at herself. Wants to give up trying* - *Worried and over-thinking. Realises what she should or should not have said* - *Negative repetitive thoughts – **'What's wrong with me?'***

Meaning: What do Finn's reactions mean?

- Unable to speak as most people do. Too slow, unsure, with a lack of social instinct.

- Can't use her previous experiences to build on future conversations as she keeps having to relearn the basics of social interactions. Sometimes the information is there and sometimes it disappears.

- Too many negative physical and mental effects to make social events fun unless with long-term friends.

Effect: How do other people react?

- Feel uncomfortable and leave as she seems to be unfriendly and aloof.

- Offended by her lack of response as they think it is because she doesn't like them.

- Impatient and frustrated at her lack of interaction and go talk to someone else.

- Continue to chat and take over the conversation to help her feel at ease.

Strategies: How can Finn deal with speaking difficulties?

- When possible, have someone who will give support in social situations that she can use as a 'social anchor' to socialise around.

- Learn techniques to manage stress – deep breathing, meditation, positive thinking.

- Start to say no to social occasions that will be too hard.

Finn's spectrum of social communication difficulties

Read Finn's creative writing. Do you think Finn's experiences of communication have a big effect on her everyday life?

What happened?

I tried to chat with some girls on my course but I was very nervous and struggling to find anything to talk about. They did a sideways shuffle to get away. I never forgot that one incident as I almost thought they were frightened of me! I've had this type of experience many times and they all made me feel that I was very strange and something was terribly wrong with me and I didn't know why.

Finn's reaction

Stage fright!
Let me dive out of sight!!
Don't open this mouth!
No words will come out!!
I've got to get as far away
as I possibly can!
Quickly!!

Finn's delayed reaction

What is wrong with me?
What is wrong with me?
It all seems too obvious now
What to say or do.
But it's too late
Again.

What Finn's reactions mean

To find the right words
Then to say them at the right time
Is a skill I don't seem to have.
I work it all out
When it is far too late
This makes me really annoyed!!
Why can't I seem to speak like everyone else?
So many times
I am misunderstood.
Regarded as cold, rude and aloof.

When I just can't speak like you!
Panic rises through my veins
As I struggle to cope
With the most basic everyday situation
Leaving an impression that I am so unfriendly.
Now I have to say that all this effort
Well it makes me extraordinarily tired!!

Other people's reactions

Often people are unsure of what to make of me with my hesitant attempts to speak. Then they do not want to find out any more and disappear in the other direction. Sometimes they will take over and lead me through the conversation, which is the best way to help me.

Finn's strategies

With a friend that I know well the nerves can disappear, as I've worked them out and I can build myself around who they are and know exactly what to say, most of the time. Somehow this bond can act as an invisible 'social anchor' holding me steady, more able to cope.

If I start to get a little nervous I can take a deep breath, counting one, two, three. With every breath leaving my body, I can let all my worries disappear until I find a quiet peace in my mind.

ACTIVITY A. YOUR WRITING PROMPTS

My spectrum of social communication difficulties

Use the following vocabulary prompts and questions to complete your worksheet and then write your own poems, thoughts, mini-stories or narrative for each topic below.

Word prompts

Social communication difficulties: Uptight, stressed, tense, stiff, awkward, hesitant, unsure, too loud or too quiet, say too little or too much, personal space, over-friendly, aloof, uncomfortable, shifty eye contact, bored, restless, acting, pretending, masking, headaches, social exhaustion, fidgeting fingers, restless feet, accepted, supported, bemused, confusion, mental effort, tired, inadequate, unwanted, excluded, lonely, over-enthusiastic, embarrassed.

Event: What happened?

How would you describe your conversational style? Think of a time when it was hard to work out what to say or what other people meant. Were you able to make eye contact or know where to stand?

Reaction: What happened in my body and mind?

Do you get totally frozen with nerves? Are you considered as someone who says too little or too much? Does your mind go blank? Do you speak easily enough but find things don't go as you expected?

Delayed reaction: What happened in my body and mind afterwards?

Do you feel exhausted or energised after socialising? Do you get a massive energy burst after being so quiet and restrained with other people? What does your body and mind need at this stage? Are you often confused after interactions?

Meaning: What do my reactions mean?

Can you work out what to say or do as easily as other people? Do you feel confident to speak but not understand social rules? Are you more comfortable being alone? How do factors such as theory of mind or processing differences affect your communication style?

How do you think it would feel when interacting with other autistic people?

Effect: How do other people react?

Do people seem patient and understanding? Are people sometimes uncomfortable with prolonged silences? Or do you find they think you are talking too much or too loud? Do people seem to misinterpret your words or behaviours?

Do you ever feel left out or ignored during social occasions? If so, do you know why this happens?

Strategies: How can I deal with speaking difficulties?

Would it help to keep a socialising monitoring chart to identify different factors that affected you and why? What would make you feel comfortable when socialising – having time limits, knowing who will be there, structured activities to focus on?

My spectrum of social communication difficulties

Record your thoughts and experiences here.

Event: What happened?

_____

_____

_____

_____

Reaction: What happened in my body and mind?

_____

_____

_____

_____

Delayed reaction: What happened in my body and mind afterwards?

_____

_____

_____

_____

Meaning: What do my reactions mean?

_____

_____

_____

_____

Effect: How do other people react?

_____

_____

_____

_____

_____

Strategies: How can I deal with speaking difficulties?

_____

_____

_____

_____

_____

This section outlines Finn's spectrum of speaking differently across different occasions. It will help you identify your own possible speaking inconsistencies.

Finn's spectrum of speaking inconsistencies

Event: What happened?

- *Finn was able to speak very well, but then the next time she met the same person she became mute and could not say one word, which caused problems.*

Reasons: Why does Finn's speaking ability change?

- *Tiredness overwhelmed and what was OK yesterday is far too hard today, even if it is only one word, as a mini-social shutdown has taken over.*

- *Her central coherence style of processing means that she has to work out what to say in each situation as she does not have an internal mental template to guide her.*

- *Her head gets stuck on intense feelings of self-consciousness, and being watched or having any kind of attention is too much to bear.*

- *Thinking of words and physically getting them out of her mouth is really hard to do sometimes.*

- *Different people lead to different reactions from Finn. Some people can be easy to speak with and others can be much more difficult for no specific reason.*

Meaning: What does this mean for Finn?

- *Embarrassed at not being able to speak properly all the time.*

- *Self-conscious about what people think of her. She can't participate the way they do so effortlessly.*

- Disheartened and overwhelmed at feeling that she cannot speak. It seems to be too much to cope with this issue every single day.

Effect: How do other people react?

- Just let it go and don't make an issue of it.

- Distrustful as she was fine yesterday, so they don't understand what the problem is today.

- Irritated at having to put up with her funny reactions and behaviour again.

- Think she is not making an effort and being cold and unfriendly rather than having a different way of communicating, even when diagnosed with autism.

Strategies: How can Finn deal with speaking inconsistencies?

- Monitor what affects her speaking ability:
  - tiredness, overwhelm, hunger, too much attention, inflexible thinking, lack of social intuition
  - tell friends and family what happens and why, so they will understand
  - recognise when she needs to be supported and when she needs to leave.

- Learn to say no to invites when she realises she will not be in a good speaking mode. Not to feel guilty as there is no point in going when she is not able to speak.

Finn's spectrum of speaking inconsistencies

Read Finn's creative writing – How do you think Finn feels when she has to deal with different situations or people that involve communication?

What happened?

I was able to speak very well on one occasion but the next time I met the same person I could not say one word. I became awkward and self-conscious and there was nothing I could do at that moment to change it or explain my behaviour.

Finn's speaking ability changes

A good speaking day is like the weather
Unpredictable, uncontrollable,
ever-changing.
With different circumstances
Leading to different results.
Confident and positive
Words may flow for a while.
Tired and feeling negative
Shutdowns quickly follow.
Mutism sets in.

Finn's speaking inconsistencies mean

Communication shutdown
I've done it again!!
Let me hide away
Until these feelings disappear.
I'm so tired of being the only one
Unable to speak on demand.

Other people's reactions

- *Well I saw her talking over there with not a trouble to be seen but now she's acting awful strange.*

- *What is wrong with her to be so sullen and cold all of a sudden without any warning?*

- *What have we done or what is her problem?*

- *She can just stay away with that attitude and atmosphere when we are having so much fun.*

Finn's speaking inconsistencies strategies

I am able to reduce the amount of speaking inconsistencies that I experience by learning to recognise the things that make me struggle and getting a feeling of what is happening in my body and mind to predict whether I will be able to speak or not. I am more able to prevent these situations that cause other people so much confusion about why I change so very much from one day to the next for no apparent reason. Though it may still happen!

ACTIVITY C. YOUR WRITING PROMPTS
My spectrum of speaking inconsistencies

Use the following vocabulary prompts and questions to complete your worksheet and then write your own poems, thoughts, mini-stories or narrative for each topic below.

Word prompts

Inconsistencies in speaking: Different circumstances, different people, mood, energy, tiredness, shutdown, meltdown, hunger, stress, preoccupied thoughts, one-track mind, overwhelm, alternative interests, pauses, hesitation, unsure, mute, mutism, inflexible, stuck, intimidated, fast conversations, slow processing, attention, choked, shyness, awkwardness, self-conscious, embarrassment, intuition, painful.

Event: What happened?

What were the circumstances that led to a change in your speaking ability?

Reasons: Why does my speaking ability change?

Are you able to generalise from one conversation to another to allow you to speak without too much extra thought? Will factors like tiredness, loss of energy or too many people affect your speaking ability?

Do new people or situations affect your speaking ability compared to familiar circumstances? Are you less able to speak within group situations?

Do you see any point in chatting to people you will never meet again?

Meaning: What does this mean for me?

Does it take you a lot of effort to work out what to say and keep speaking? How does your inconsistent speaking ability affect relationships/friendships?

Do you sometimes feel like you are constantly failing? Does it seem like you are being uncooperative rather than not able to sustain a constant level of interaction?

Effect: How do other people react?

Do people seem to question your behaviour? Would they try to include you even if you're not speaking as expected? Do they get annoyed or suspicious and think you are doing it on purpose? Does your withdrawal, silence or stilted speaking style make them think you don't like them?

Strategies: How can I deal with speaking inconsistencies?

Would it help if you had extra time to think of what to say? Would having set time alone give you the boost needed to begin participating again? Are you able to communicate via text or online to reduce social demands?

Do you just need to have any speaking inconsistencies accepted with less pressure to meet others' expectations all the time?

My spectrum of speaking inconsistencies

Record your thoughts and experiences here.

Event: What happened?

_____

_____

_____

_____

Reasons: Why does my speaking ability change?

_____

_____

_____

_____

Meaning: What does this mean for me?

_____

_____

_____

_____

Effect: How do other people react?

_____

_____

_____

_____

Strategies: How can I deal with speaking inconsistencies?

_____

_____

_____

_____

This section outlines Finn's spectrum of making friends. It will help you identify your own profile of making friends.

Finn's spectrum of making friends

Event: What happened?

- Someone wanted to talk to her to make friends, but she avoided them rather than deal with it as it was too much hard work and she was tired and can never guarantee to be able to speak well the next time they meet. It might get awkward.

Reaction: How does Finn react to people trying to make friends with her?

- Wants to hide and avoid trying to make friends.

- Appears distant and preoccupied to avoid having to talk.

- Leaves early to avoid getting caught up in conversations as they might find out how badly she speaks.

Meaning: What do Finn's reactions mean?

- She feels like she can't speak, which stops her from trying to interact and make friends as there are so many aspects of socialising that are difficult to work out and it tires her out really quickly.

- She does not know what to say or do, so it is easier to stay on her own. Sometimes when she does speak it seems to go very wrong as she is remarkably blunt.

- Loss of confidence in her ability to make and keep friends; she wonders why anyone would want to be friends with her anyway.

- Problems speaking consistently mean that she is afraid to try as she can't guarantee she will be able to speak as well the next time.

Effect: How do other people react?

- *Disdainful or bemused at her silence and lack of interaction, leaving them uninterested in talking to her.*

- *Don't notice she is there.*

- *Happy to include her even when she is very, very quiet.*

Strategies: What would help Finn to make friends?

- *A friend to accompany her when meeting new people as she will be able to frame herself around the person she knows and build up new relationships from this point.*

- *When other people talk a lot and they take the lead, while including her without expectations or judgement.*

- *Enough time to watch and learn how to speak to each person by finding out about their background and type of personality.*

- *Find interests in common with other people that will help to keep the conversation flowing.*

Finn's spectrum of making friends

Read Finn's creative writing. How might having difficulty making friends make Finn feel?

What happened?

I realised that someone was heading in my direction and knew they wanted to be friends. But that would be tricky to negotiate without someone else I already know beside me to build my conversations around. I must get out of the way right now.

Finn's reactions to people trying to make friends with her

Every time someone seems to be heading towards me I have an automatic reaction to panic. It doesn't matter who they are, it's nothing to do with them. I simply find it overwhelming to stay and try to chat.

What Finn's reactions mean

Simple interactions
Create complications.
Speaking inconsistencies

Make me give up.
If I speak well today
What will happen the next time we meet?

Other people's reactions

Reactions can be mixed
Supportive and kind
Accepting and including
From those who don't seem to judge

With sniggers and comments
Boredom and irritation
From those who have no time for me.
And it's me that is considered to be rude!

Finn's strategies to make friends

No judgements or annoyance
At the lack of interaction.

Being allowed to stay quiet
Without any need for explanation
Until I have some time to sit back and watch
To let my understanding of a person grow.

Common interests and passions
Will always help the conversation flow.
With focused activities to take part in
I can keep my hands and mind constructively occupied.

All these things will help me make connections,
Build friendships to last.

ACTIVITY E. YOUR WRITING PROMPTS

My spectrum of making friends

Use the following vocabulary prompts and questions to complete your worksheet and then write your own poems, thoughts, mini-stories or narrative for each topic below.

Word prompts

Making friends: Mono-syllabic response, confident, self-assured, nervous, fearful, blunt, honest, to the point, straightforward, factual, accurate, give lots of detail or information, mumbles, blank mind, uninterested in typical conversations, awkward, stilted, unsure, lost, copying people, subdued, withdrawn, over-enthusiastic, eager, too friendly, staring/hesitant eye contact, loud, forward, opinionated, knowledgeable, informative.

Event: What happened?

What type of situation were you in when trying to make friends?

Did you approach the other person or did they? Was it a positive or negative experience?

Reaction: How do I react to people trying to make friends with me?

Do you withdraw and become distant, trying to appear uninterested to hide your fears? Are you very enthusiastic and want to tell them everything about yourself? Does this work?

Will you try to chat and think it is going well but somehow a friendship doesn't develop?

Meaning: What do my reactions mean?

Are people difficult to connect with no matter how hard you try? Do you get overwhelmed with nerves and tension trying to socialise? Is this obvious to other people or hidden inside you? Is it easier to stay away from people and not try to make friends? Do you find that you put so much effort into making friends that it might seem to be too much for other people's expectations?

Effect: How do other people react?

Do people seem to feel uncomfortable and withdraw? Are people confused by your responses or behaviours – too quiet or speaking a lot, unexpected responses? Will they support you if they can see you are struggling or explain things?

Strategies: What would help me to make friends?

Would it be useful to get to know someone online before meeting them in person? If you do, then it is essential to be cautious about any friendship that you make on the internet. People can pretend to be someone they are not when interacting online. With autism we tend to believe what people say without questioning their motives. This means that we might be at a greater risk of believing what someone says and possibly being taken advantage of. It might be a good idea if your parents could monitor any new friends made through the internet.

Could you join a club to help build relationships through common interests? Would you be more comfortable if this was with other autistic teenagers?

ACTIVITY F. MY WORKSHEET

My spectrum of making friends

Record your thoughts and experiences here.

Event: What happened?

_____

_____

_____

_____

Reaction: How do I react to people trying to make friends with me?

_____

_____

_____

_____

Meaning: What do my reactions mean?

_____

_____

_____

_____

Effect: How do other people react?

_____

_____

_____

_____

Strategies: What would help me to make friends?

_____

_____

_____

_____

This section outlines Finn's spectrum of social burnout. It will help you identify your own experiences of social burnout.

Finn's spectrum of social burnout

Event: What happened?

- *Finn took part in a social occasion and now she is exhausted and has shut down.*

Reaction: How does social burnout feel in Finn's body and mind?

Body	Mind
• *Can't say one syllable*	• *Closed down*
• *Exhaustion*	• *Blank*
• *Autopilot*	• *Can't bear to hear a voice*
• *Feels sick*	• *Pain*
• *Hesitant eye contact/words*	• *Unable to think – mono-processing*
• *Nervous tension*	• *Unable to react*
	• *Needs to be alone*

Meaning: What did Finn's reactions mean?

- *Couldn't cope with a typical social occasion.*

- *Finds it hard to be around people for a long time as she does not have as much social energy as other people.*

- *Her body and brain no longer work when drained from being out for a long time with people.*

- *Difficulty working out how much she can cope with to prevent a communication shutdown.*

Effect: How do other people react?

- Tried to keep conversations going without any negative feelings towards her.

- Let her remain silent without any expectations.

- Don't notice her inability to speak. Thought she was being rude and immature.

- Made up their own reasons why she was not speaking or participating and withdrew.

- Carried on as normal and let her recover the ability to speak without deciding why she was acting that way.

Strategies: What would stop Finn having a socialising shutdown?

- Planning social occasions so she can prepare and work out how long she can cope with them.

- Sleep, food, space, less demands, less people and noise.

- Not taking part in events when she is too tired to cope.

- Regular breaks from standing around for a long time with lots of talking.

- One-to-one conversations rather than groups of people.

Finn's spectrum of social burnout

Read Finn's creative writing. Do you think experiencing social burnouts would affect Finn's relationships with other people?

What happened?

Socialising takes a toll, drains my body, tires my brain, social burnout quickly follows, no more social talk will happen.

Finn's social burnout

So much talking, chattering, animated enthusiasm falls flat inside my head. It crumbles up my brain until I can no longer think, speak or move a single, tiny muscle from all this social stuff that takes 100% effort just to sit through it. After all that I am very, very tired, which means that now is not the time to talk to me!!

What Finn's reactions mean

I don't understand how you can talk so easily
Without ever seeming to need to think.
It makes me so tired
My head has to shut down.
Then all I can do is mumble
One half word at a time.
Which makes you grumble...
Can you not speak right!!
No I cannot speak!
I am mute!!

Other people's reactions

Some people are kind
Giving time and space automatically
Without really knowing why it's needed
They just do it and it's so helpful.
This lets me recover and begin again
Without any feelings of blame.

Other people are judgemental
Irritation follows misunderstandings.
Presumptions and assumptions
Of my behaviours & lack of interaction.
With no questions or any interest
About what is happening inside me
To cause this communication shutdown.

Finn's strategies to prevent social burnout

Sleep, food and time out.
Support, acceptance, understanding.
No explanations required.

No expectations that I can't meet.
Knowing my limits.
An escape plan for all occasions!!!

ACTIVITY G. YOUR WRITING PROMPTS

My spectrum of social burnout

Use the following vocabulary prompts and questions to complete your worksheet and then write your own poems, thoughts, mini-stories or narrative for each topic below.

Word prompts

Social burnout: Exhaustion, blank, static, swamped, drained, shutdown, mute, bored, distant, cold, aloof, strained, irritated, uncomfortable, frustrated, sad, limits, stretched beyond my capacity, painful, prickly, spiky, sharp, snappy, scowling, exhaustion, distressing, gloomy, touchy, crabby, short-tempered, tetchy, grouchy, disorientated, dazed, muddled, numb, emotionless, passive, detached.

Event: What happened?

What happened before and/or during the social occasion to cause a physical and mental burnout to happen?

Reaction: How does social burnout feel in my body and mind?

Do you feel drained and exhausted, unable to say anything with huge effort? Does your body feel heavy and weak? What thoughts go through your mind? How do you react to other people talking to you?

Meaning: What did my reactions mean?

Are you able to function to the same extent as other people? Does it feel like you have a completely different socialising system compared to everyone else? Is socialising hard work to sustain? Do your body and mind switch off at a certain point? Is there any point in people trying to talk to you when you are socially burnt out?

Effect: How do other people react?

Are people aggravated by what they view as poor behaviour? Will they try to find out what would help you cope better? Does anyone offer words of encouragement? Do they ignore you?

Strategies: What would stop me from having a socialising shutdown?

Would you find it helpful to have warnings of events – who will be there, when it will be over? If you were able to come and go to suit your socialising needs, would that allow you to cope better? Would controlling how many people or new situations you have to deal with prevent this from happening too often?

How much time out would you need to recover from social burnout? Can you monitor the things that cause you to lose social energy – eating regularly, too many people, tiredness, not knowing what will happen?

My spectrum of social burnout

Record your thoughts and experiences here.

Event: What happened?

_____

_____

_____

_____

_____

Reaction: How does social burnout feel in my body and mind?

_____

_____

_____

_____

_____

Meaning: What did my reactions mean?

_____

_____

_____

_____

_____

Effect: How do other people react?

_____

_____

_____

_____

_____

Strategies: What would stop me from having a socialising shutdown?

_____

_____

_____

_____

_____

This section provides a summary of Finn's social communication profile. Read through it and use all the information you have learnt about your spectrum of social communication throughout this chapter to create your own version.

What's Finn's spectrum of social communication?

Finn feels comfortable speaking when:

- amongst other autistic people
- with people she knows very well and who accept her even when silent
- with people who have shared interests
- in a good mood and feeling energetic
- aware of what is expected with no pressure to comply.

Finn finds it hard to speak when:

- she doesn't know what she is supposed to say
- tired or stressed, shutdown and switched off. She becomes mute even with friends
- meeting the same acquaintances on a continuous basis – lunchtime, breaktime
- being watched and feeling self-conscious
- attending social events, classes, work, in groups, most places!
- in situations that don't give her time to watch people and figure out what to talk about with them...which may still only last a short while!
- speaking difficulties are always a constant theme in her life; they cause her the most hassle and stress out of everything that is part of her autism spectrum.

To be able to speak well Finn needs to:

- *feel that she is accepted whether too quiet or too blunt*
- *be allowed to speak or remain silent without pressure to conform*
- *have no impatient questions, sudden demands or negative comments*
- *be given some time to absorb the information and prepare to think of some words*
- *have time out to decompress, recover and rest.*

Finn would like other people to:

- *accept that her speaking inconsistencies are genuine*
- *act as a supportive friend that she can interact with and rely on when socialising*
- *give her extra time to process what they have said and think of what to say in response*
- *let her sit back and watch so she can figure them out before trying to build a friendship*
- *not make assumptions about why she is not speaking*
- *let her make mistakes and not judge especially when she is quiet*
- *not take what she is saying or not saying personally*
- *let her communicate through writing, texts, e-mail. Avoid unexpected phone calls!*

ACTIVITY I. MY WORKSHEET

What's my spectrum of social communication?

Record your thoughts and experiences here.

I feel comfortable speaking when:

_____

_____

_____

I find it hard to speak when:

_____

_____

_____

To be able to speak well I need to:

_____

_____

_____

I would like other people to:

_____

_____

_____

What's Finn's spectrum of social communication?

Read Finn's poem and consider what similarities or differences you have with Finn's thoughts on social communication.

Words

The words struggle out
As I choke speak.
Leaves me a stranger
To those I am beside.

You think you know what that means.
How it translates across time.

But I have no words to take you
To the places I know
When I am once more
On my own.

So will I leave as I arrived?
Unheard.

Or will you listen
Beyond silence
To the words on the other side

What's my spectrum of social communication?

Record your poems, thoughts or mini-stories here.

Why don't you write a poem or a story about:

- your communication style and experiences

- what you would like to develop

- what you would like other people to know about your spectrum of social communication?

_____

_____

_____

_____

_____

_____

_____

_____

_____

_____

ACTIVITY K. MY PROFILE CHART

My social communication profile

Strengths	Challenges
•	•
•	•
•	•
•	•
•	•

Strategies	Goals
•	•
•	•
•	•
•	•
•	•

Top three things you need to know about me

•

•

•

Chapter 6

Know Your Spectrum of Shutdowns and Meltdowns

Introduction

Triggers

Being autistic means that we can experience shutdowns and meltdowns. Shutdowns and meltdowns can happen for lots of reasons, including tiredness, emotional or social burnout, stress, feeling overwhelmed, information or sensory overload, or problems in our lives that we find hard to cope with. While other people's bodies and minds have the same underlying reactions and feelings, an autistic person's responses tend to be either much more or much less intense. Having a shutdown or meltdown would be considered an intense reaction.

As our sensory systems can be more sensitive to noises, touch, lights and many other external stimuli, we can be affected by everyday life in a way that other people are not. Our processing differences also mean that we have different ways of reacting and behaving.

The potential influence of our executive functioning style may also act as an additional trigger. Our rigid style of thinking might mean we have difficulty stopping activities, which could lead to a total state of exhaustion as we keep working or socialising even when our body or mind is hurting. We ignore the warning signs so that we can finish off tasks as we are absolutely focused on getting to the end and completing everything we set out to do until we reach the point of a shutdown. We might also be perfectionists, and if something is not quite right then this might cause a mini-meltdown if we can't cope with making a mistake.

Difficulty in realising when we need help can mean that it is not always obvious to us that we are in trouble. When we do get to the point of knowing that we need help, it might not necessarily occur to us to actually ask someone to give us help, or we may not be able to work out who to turn to or how to express our needs verbally (Attwood 2008).

Confusion within our interoception system may further affect our ability to regulate our bodies as we may not register that we are hungry, tired, sick or in pain. This could lead to us continuing activities and reaching a point where we cannot cope as we are suddenly submerged in feelings of hunger or tiredness that we did not notice building up until it was too late.

Too many social demands might leave us in a state of burnout and we need to withdraw from any social activities. We may be unable to communicate our needs effectively to explain what happens to us, especially during the actual shutdown or meltdown process.

Emotional confusion or distress may turn into a shutdown or meltdown if we are unable to recognise and manage our internal feelings, which can be something people with autism find difficult. Our feelings might build up inside us until we become overwhelmed. In addition we might not have the communication skills to express our emotions constructively, or the social support to help us cope with any difficulties we are experiencing.

Our ability to deal with these triggers can change across time and circumstances, with our responses ranging from being hyposensitive to hypersensitive (i.e. under- or over-sensitive). We may not react in one situation as our system is under-sensitive, but another time, due to many factors, we might become more sensitive and shut down or have a meltdown (Bogdashina 2016). These changes in our sensitivity to sensory information mean that we might not notice and appear unresponsive to a sound, but the next day we overreact to the same noise as it is now hurting our ears (Bogdashina 2016).

When we are overloaded with too much information, we close off parts of our processing channels to adjust how much external information gets through in order to allow our bodies and minds to cope (Bogdashina 2016).

It might take us a long time to enter into a state of shutdown or meltdown and it is hard to identify what is happening, or it could be quite sudden without any warning (Bogdashina 2016). Each of us will have our own set of limits, and the speed at which shutdown or meltdown happens will be affected by our own individual capacity to cope with whatever is causing us problems.

Shutdowns

A shutdown is when we temporarily lose the ability to speak, interact and sometimes to function at all. This is an internal reaction and other people can't see what is happening underneath the surface. It can appear that we are being rude or ignoring people rather than experiencing a loss of functioning and needing to withdraw. We can zone out and switch off, becoming unresponsive for a while, and we can no longer participate. Our bodies might feel extremely tired and we can become mute, losing the ability to speak. Making eye contact could feel painful. Our perception may become more distorted so that our movements, vision and hearing change, making it hard to recognise familiar things and perform physical actions (Bogdashina 2016).

A shutdown can take many forms, and our responses will be based on our individual way of coping with different types of overwhelm or overload.

Temporary shutdown

A shutdown might mean that we focus all our energy on processing different feelings, thoughts or sensory sensations, but lose the ability to respond so we can't speak or react. Or a temporary shutdown will reduce awareness of our bodies through our senses – vision, hearing, touch, taste, smell. It can involve one or more sensory channels closing over, which means we begin to mono-process information on one or only a couple of sensory channels. The process of temporarily shutting down allows us to keep functioning, but using only a limited number of senses which can now work better (Bogdashina 2016).

Total shutdown

We might experience a total shutdown which results in sensory agnosia. This means we might keep our visual and hearing senses open and be able to see or hear information, but our brains are not processing what the words or images mean, as our ability to reason has shut down. We are operating on autopilot – moving and acting without interpreting and thinking about what we are doing. It can seem as if we are blind or deaf or not know what our body is doing (Bogdashina 2016). We might mindlessly follow people and become disorientated and forget how to move our body (Bogdashina 2016).

Partial shutdown

We can also have a partial shutdown, which means we can only feel part of a touch or hear parts of speech. We might find that we live in a permanent state of partial shutdown as a way of coping with our environment. This means we are able to function and keep doing things, but with a reduced awareness of what is around us. When we are in a shutdown we might not respond to our names being called, notice other people in a room or react to smells or touch (Bogdashina 2016).

Meltdowns

A meltdown tends to be an external reaction and can be misinterpreted as bad behaviour rather than an inability to cope with what has happened or what is affecting us. Having a meltdown means that we might cry, scream, hurt ourselves and lose the ability to think logically. Sometimes meltdowns can be internal and we don't make any sounds or actions to show that we are in a state of meltdown; we are quietly disintegrating inside, but mute on the outside.

Most of the time other people don't realise how everyday activities affect us or the differences in how our bodies and minds work. They may not know that we are having difficulty processing information and that we are unable to respond or continue as expected. It can seem that we are acting this way on purpose and being cold, distant, bad-tempered or unfriendly. If people don't understand what is happening they might take our behaviours personally and think we are withdrawing or overreacting because of them.

Through learning to recognise how we function, we can help other people to understand what it means to have a different processing system.

It is also important for us that we are aware of how we function so that we can be more in control of our behaviours. If we can identify the triggers that cause our shutdowns and meltdowns we can begin to manage how often they happen and learn to develop strategies to cope.

Understanding our experiences of shutdowns and meltdowns will help to improve our relationships and we will hopefully feel more balanced within our bodies and minds in our everyday lives.

This section outlines Finn's spectrum of shutdowns. It will help you identify your own profile of experiencing shutdowns.

Finn's spectrum of shutdowns

Event: What happened?

Finn was doing lots of jobs and, due to her rigid thinking style, she had difficulty changing her course of action once she had started and wouldn't stop until she had finished. She was physically exhausted, leading to a temporary shutdown so she could no longer talk or take part in any social interactions. However, she was in the middle of a social event when this happened.

Reaction: What happened in Finn's body and mind?

Body	Mind
• *Too many sounds and voices hurt* • *Heavy, slow* • *Touch irritates* • *Effortful, feels like she is crawling through* • *Mute, unresponsive, snappy* • *Can only focus on what she is doing to be able to function* • *Lights irritate*	• *Blank, no thoughts, blurred awareness* • *Tired, drained, empty, slow* • *Mono-processing – words, actions* • *Speaking irritates, responses are impossible* • *Microscopic perception/awareness* • *Overwhelmed, closed off, withdrawn, cold, prickly*

Delayed reaction: What happened in Finn's body and mind afterwards?

- Her body retreated. Her mind closed down. Recovery time means being left alone. Or she will have a very cold response to any approaches to speak, no matter how simple.

- Embarrassed at being unable to speak or cope with everyday stuff and never learning when to stop.

- Feeling physically ill and really frustrated at being unable to effectively monitor her activities and recognise when she needs to stop, regardless of what she has decided to complete. Fully aware that she will do it again!

- Annoyed at herself for not being more prepared and avoiding any social contact until she was able to handle it.

Meaning: What did Finn's reactions mean?

- Sometimes unable to cope with the same demands as other people, but a great capacity to work for long periods of time without a break.

- Lack of awareness of changes in her body and inability to predict how they will develop mean it didn't occur to her that she was too tired and hungry and she was at risk of shutting down.

- Ineffective strategies to change her focus, recognise when she needs to stop and adapt plans according to her physical and mental needs.

Effect: How did other people react?

- Annoyed at her attitude as she should be talking and joining in like everyone else.

- Moved away to avoid being around her.

- Carried on as if she was not there.

- Stopped and checked if they could help, then gave her space and time alone to recover.

Strategies: How could Finn prevent a shutdown?

- *Explain to other people what happens when she is very tired before it happens. Let them know it is not personal.*

- *Create a hand signal to show others when she needs to be left alone without any further need to explain at that moment of shutdown.*

- *Plan to avoid a shutdown through developing awareness of physical and mental warning signs and taking preventative action – 3Qs (see Finn's creative writing, below).*

- *Avoid too many social demands, especially when she knows tiredness will be a problem.*

Finn's spectrum of shutdowns

Read Finn's creative writing. Do you think Finn finds shutdowns difficult to control?

What happened?

Ten hours of working straight through leaves me without words. Shutdown slowly takes hold. It's out of my control. Conversational chatter passes me by. Quizzically raised eyebrows that don't understand. Shutdowns happen all the time.

Finn's reactions

Sounds pierce my head,
A touch hurts my skin,
My brain overwhelmed,
Leaves my body in pain,
Words are lost,
I need to be alone.

Finn's delayed reaction

Frustration surrounds my total inability to stop and think about what will happen next, how I will feel in two hours' time, maybe I should take a break.
  I should have known to stay away, avoid all contact, until I could cope. Now all I can do is feel out of my depth. Or hold up a warning sign... Don't bother speaking to me right now!

What Finn's reactions mean

Shutdowns are one of my biggest difficulties to manage and cope with. A major cause of my shutdowns is deciding on a course of action and not stopping until it is completed. The time, the effort, whatever it takes, does not matter to me. I only see the end target point and I will not stop. My mind goes in very straight lines and I just keep going. Then when I have finished and stop to look around, feeling pride in all that I have done, a slow *realisation creeps over me. I am ready to collapse! Rapidly followed with my total submersion into a temporary shutdown. Then I think to myself, I will do better next time...*

Other people's reactions

What's wrong with you?
Stop acting up!
Are you not too old for all that?
Being so rude!
How can I help?

Finn's shutdown prevention strategy

3Qs

- *How do my body and mind feel?*
- *Can I cope with what I have to do?*
- *How will I feel in five hours if I don't stop now?*

My spectrum of shutdowns

Use the following vocabulary prompts and questions to complete your worksheet and then write your own poems, thoughts, mini-stories or narrative for each topic below.

Word prompts

Shutdowns: Withdraw, silent, jagged, prickly, spiky, brain freeze, overwhelmed, aloof, cold, exhausted, mute, blank, motionless, mono-processing, mono-syllabic, invaded, pain, rituals, rocking, pacing, glazed, vacant, expressionless, sensitive, heightened, meaningless, overload, stretched, hyper/hypo reactions, autopilot, snappy, mono-responses.

Event: What happened?

What caused the shutdown – socialising, sensory, tiredness, hunger, did too much work?

Were there any warning signs – rocking, stillness, silence, irritation, pacing?

Reaction: What happened in my body and mind?

How does your body feel during a shutdown? Is it tense, heavy or achy? Do you notice things like noises less or more intensely? What thoughts go through your mind? Are you able to talk? Can your body continue to function on autopilot without thinking?

Delayed reaction: What happened in my body and mind afterwards?

What feelings do you have after experiencing a shutdown? Do you feel good about yourself or negative? How does your body react? Are you tired and need to switch off mentally?

Meaning: What did my reactions mean?

Do you lose energy to cope with people or places when you have a shutdown? Are there any warning signs that usually happen before a shutdown – rocking or pacing? Do you tend to become very withdrawn and silent but appear 'fine' to other people? Are you able to monitor your needs to prevent shutdowns?

Effect: How did other people react?

What do people think of your behaviours? Do shutdowns create barriers with family and friends? Would many people understand that you need some space and time to recover?

Strategies: How could I prevent a shutdown?

Think about what your biggest triggers are and how you could manage them.

Would it be useful if you had a visual record of shutdown triggers and warning signs to check if you need to withdraw? Are scheduled plans helpful to reduce the stress of not knowing what will happen?

My spectrum of shutdowns

Record your thoughts and experiences here.

Event: What happened?

_____

_____

_____

_____

Reaction: What happened in my body and mind?

_____

_____

_____

_____

Delayed reaction: What happened in my body and mind afterwards?

_____

_____

_____

_____

Meaning: What did my reactions mean?

_____

_____

_____

_____

Effect: How did other people react?

_____

_____

_____

_____

Strategies: How could I prevent a shutdown?

_____

_____

_____

_____

This section outlines Finn's spectrum of partial shutdowns. It will help you identify your own profile of experiencing a partial shutdown.

Finn's spectrum of partial shutdowns

Event: What happened?

- *Finn can be partially shut down and switched off from things a lot of the time and not notice until someone points out to her that she has walked straight past them or not responded to her name.*

Reasons: Why does Finn have partial shutdowns?

- *Too much noise hurts her head and she needs an escape.*

- *Becomes hyper-focused on whatever she is thinking about and automatically tunes out from external distractions.*

- *Too much socialising means she will glaze over, blank out conversations and not be able to think or talk any more.*

Effect: How do other people react?

- *Think she is ignoring them on purpose.*

- *Wonder what is in her mind.*

- *Not really notice anything different unless she does not respond.*

Strategies: How can Finn deal with partial shutdowns?

- *As it is a positive way of allowing her to function and preventing overload, just make sure there are no physical risks for her or others from not hearing sounds or noticing people.*

- *Develop a prompt system for other people to point out if she seems to be distant and not absorbing things so she can be aware when it is happening and identify triggers.*

Finn's spectrum of partial shutdowns

Read Finn's poem. Are partial shutdowns a problem for Finn or something that is useful, or both?

Finn's partial shutdown

Partial shutdown
Is a familiar thing
It helps my mind
To keep nice and calm
I flick a switch
Without even knowing
My head shuts down
My body keeps going.
It lets me ignore
All those irritating noises
That hurt my ears
Make me feel like screaming!

Now I've got a chance
To focus on my thoughts
But people sometimes think
This is something to address
'Cause it seems I'm being rude
When I walk straight past them
Not even hearing their words when they call me by my name!
When all that is really happening is that I am partially shutdown.

ACTIVITY C. YOUR WRITING PROMPTS

My spectrum of partial shutdowns

Use the following vocabulary prompts and questions to complete your worksheet and then write your own poems, thoughts, mini-stories or narrative for each topic below.

Word prompts

Partial shutdowns: Risks, reduced, narrowed perception, fragment, constricted, temporary, permanent, continuous, mild, severe, deaf, hearing loss, muffled, narrowed vision, blind, visual, touch, no physical sensation, numb, switch-off, unresponsive, indifferent, rude, ignore, disregard, distracted, function, sustainable, bearable, maintain, safety, automatic.

Event: What happened?

Are you aware of being partially shutdown? Which sense or senses seem to switch off to allow you to continue to do things? Do you think you experience partial shutdowns a lot of the time?

Reasons: Why do I have partial shutdowns?

What causes partial shutdowns to happen – is it sensory overload and you need to reduce the impact? Does your perception of objects or people become fragmented into separate parts as there is too much information to absorb and work out all at once?

Do you have to avoid eye contact as it might be painful? Do you not hear people's questions as too much noise has made your ears shut down? If someone touches you, can you always feel it? If not, why does this happen?

Effect: How do other people react?

Does anyone realise this can happen to you or that it might be a permanent way of dealing with everyday life? Is this something you can see in other people in your family?

Do people accept your reactions or understand that it is part of autism? Can it cause laughter, arguments or confusion?

Strategies: How can I deal with partial shutdowns?

Would it be useful to reduce sensory factors that cause this to happen? How can you work out when this is happening and when you need support with it?

How can you help other people to understand that it is a protective reaction that helps you to cope better?

My spectrum of partial shutdowns

Record your thoughts and experiences here.

Event: What happened?

_____

_____

_____

Reasons: Why do I have partial shutdowns?

_____

_____

_____

Effect: How do other people react?

_____

_____

_____

Strategies: How can I deal with partial shutdowns?

_____

_____

_____

This section outlines Finn's spectrum of experiencing a meltdown. It will help you identify your own profile of experiencing a meltdown.

Finn's spectrum of meltdowns

Event: What happened?

Finn was unable to manage her emotions as she became overwhelmed thinking about lots of different things that had gone wrong, things she had done and other people's actions too.

Reaction: What happened in Finn's body and mind?

Body	Mind
• Energy surge • Hitting her head • Shoulder and neck tension • Sick, nervous energy • Banging body against walls • Silent aggression • Pacing • Rocking	• Frustration, agitation, distress, anger, total overwhelm • Black and white rigid thinking, everything is bad... • Exploding with thoughts – can't stop thinking • Repetitive negative thoughts, darkness, blackness • Arguing in her head, no words to say, or too many • Balanced communication is not possible • Unable to rationalize events and see positives • Can't deal with multiple difficulties at once • Can't see options or solutions

Delayed reaction: What happened in Finn's body and mind afterwards?

- *Drained exhaustion leaves her body motionless as she collapses in tears.*

- *Despair disappears as weariness takes hold. She can no longer feel anything.*

- *Sleep takes over as there is nothing more she can think or do.*

Meaning: What did Finn's reactions mean?

- *Difficulties expressing her emotions in a constructive way.*

- *Emotional processing of events may be delayed but then all her feelings will overwhelm her and her mind will jump from one topic to another.*

- *Underdeveloped outlets for her emotions reduce her coping skills.*

- *Rigid thinking means that she will hyper-focus on individual issues in a repetitive sequence.*

- *Inflexible thinking style prevents her from identifying a range of options, which makes things seem insurmountable.*

Effect: How did other people react?

- *Finn only ever has meltdowns when she is on her own, usually at 3 am. Her processing is delayed and she holds things in until she can be alone and then it all overwhelms her.*

Strategies: How can Finn prevent meltdowns?

- *Identify what she can cope with and what she needs help with and plan to avoid meltdown triggers.*

- *Bullet-point her repetitive thoughts and identify what effect they have on her reactions.*

- *Work out a system to express her emotions in smaller stages and learn to deal with things in gradual steps.*

- *Use music, films, books, exercise to release emotions before they build up.*

Finn's spectrum of meltdowns

Read Finn's creative writing. How do you think Finn will feel after a meltdown?

What happened?

Emotions cause trouble; they pile up in a queue. I can't seem to work them out or deal with them effectively. One minute I am fine, the next, I can hardly breathe. Meltdowns don't happen too often to me.

Finn's reaction

Tension. Pacing. Words spit out inside my head. Options vanish. I see only things that make me angry or sad. The wall is my opponent until the tears take over.

Finn's delayed reaction

Sleep pulls me in, thoughts start to crumble. My body's done in.

What Finn's reactions mean

Emotions are tough, they mostly confuse, it seems I've got it sorted, everything's under control. Until...BAM, they hit, with one hard blow. Details magnified, single problems multiply. I fall into the blackest hole of depression in a rapidly expanding spiral, spinning faster and faster out of control.

Other people's reactions

I keep it to myself, never show when I'm upset; it seems I might feel nothing much, but inside I'm all tied up, twisted tight in knots.

Finn's meltdown prevention strategies

- *Identify causes* – emotional overwhelm, routines, frustration
- *Manage triggers*
  - *Express emotions* – write, draw, sing, move
  - *Routine* – support from others by giving warnings and preparation for changes
- *Restorative strategies* – deep pressure, music, time alone, writing, sleeping, exercise, interests

ACTIVITY E. YOUR WRITING PROMPTS

My spectrum of meltdowns

Use the following vocabulary prompts and questions to complete your worksheet and then write your own poems, thoughts, mini-stories or narrative for each topic below.

Word prompts

Body meltdown: Bursting, scream, head crashes, hurt, hair pulling, fuzzy, tightened, squeezed, stiffened, constricted, self-harm, biting, hitting, scratching, banging, energy burst, energy crash, fatigue, tears, pain, release, trapped, uncommunicative, hostile, aggressive, deep body pressure.

Mind meltdown: Agitated, foggy thinking, confused, rigid, inflexible, focused, stuck, periscope view/perspective, derailed, scattered, incoherent, anger, self-regulation, under attack, shame, isolating, uncontrollable, misunderstood, self-hatred, overpowering, uncontainable, pressure, trapped, submerged, black, absolute overwhelm, internal, adaptability, intense, withdrawal.

Event: What happened?

What were the triggers for your meltdown – sensory overload, social or emotional overwhelm, unexpected changes, lack of routine, inability to communicate needs, an argument, being bullied, feeling bad about yourself, being blamed or judged, confusion?

Reaction: What happened in my body and mind?

What physical sensations do you have? Does your body feel tense, restless, agitated? Will your thoughts become overwhelmingly negative? Do you ever do anything to hurt yourself to release these feelings?

Delayed reaction: What happened in my body and mind afterwards?

What kind of feelings do you experience when the meltdown is over? Are you embarrassed and full of regret? Do you need time on your own? Are you exhausted but unable to sleep with too many feelings swirling around inside?

Meaning: What did my reactions mean?

Do you need to make everything stop? What are your meltdown triggers? Are sensory sensitivities a factor in your meltdowns? What impact will your emotions have on a meltdown? At what point are you unable to prevent a meltdown?

Effect: How did other people react?

Do people notice that you are experiencing a meltdown? Will they think it is due to some other reason? Do they think it is a negative reaction?

Would many people understand and accept this is a temporary but natural reaction for someone with autism or would they think it is strange? Do they try to help by using deep pressure or any other strategy to release the meltdown energy and emotions?

Strategies: How can I prevent meltdowns?

What triggers in your daily life could you learn to manage to reduce the amount of meltdowns – lack of food, sleep or physical movement?

Would it help to learn to monitor your emotions using a mood journal to recognise when you might be at risk of overwhelm?

Are you able to control your exposure to any sensory factors that cause your meltdowns?

My spectrum of meltdowns

Record your thoughts and experiences here.

Event: What happened?

_____

_____

_____

_____

Reaction: What happened in my body and mind?

_____

_____

_____

_____

Delayed reaction: What happened in my body and mind afterwards?

_____

_____

_____

_____

Meaning: What did my reactions mean?

_____

_____

_____

_____

Effect: How did other people react?

_____

_____

_____

_____

Strategies: How can I prevent meltdowns?

_____

_____

_____

_____

This section provides a summary of Finn's shutdown and meltdown profile. Read through it and use all the information you have learnt about your spectrum of shutdowns and meltdowns throughout this chapter to create your own version.

What's Finn's spectrum of shutdowns and meltdowns?

Triggers: Finn may shut down or have a meltdown when:

- socialising for too long
- under pressure to speak
- stressed and overwhelmed by people, events or situations
- hearing too many noises from all different directions
- having to deal with several things at once
- hungry, tired or she has done too much exercise or activities
- overwhelmed with emotions that she may not be able to fully process or recognise.
- she does not realise that she needs help to deal with her emotions

To prevent a shutdown or a meltdown Finn needs to:

- eat, exercise and sleep well
- spend time pursuing her interests or routines on her own
- plan events in advance so she knows what is expected, with the option to withdraw at any time without explanation
- work out how much time she can spend with people
- learn to recognise her triggers and recognise when a shutdown/meltdown is starting to happen.

Finn is able to cope when:

- emotions are monitored and expressed constructively through music, activities, writing

- in control of what she has to do

- given time alone when she needs to withdraw

- able to make choices about what she is able to cope with at each stage of events

- aware of her partial shutdowns and any risk they might cause.

Finn would like other people to:

- be understanding that her needs in relation to autism are real

- let her have time on her own without thinking it is a negative thing

- make allowances for her routines and interests to be followed

- know that she has difficulty understanding and processing her emotions

- understand that her processing of issues may be delayed and fragmented

- not take her shutdown behaviour/reactions personally

- not judge or comment when she is extraordinarily quiet

- appreciate that her ability to cope changes with tiredness, hunger, stress

- know she can't always predict how she will react until it is too late

- support her when she is unable to continue as expected.

What's my spectrum of shutdowns and meltdowns?

Record your thoughts and experiences here.

Triggers: I may shut down or have a meltdown when:

_____

_____

_____

_____

_____

To prevent a shutdown or a meltdown I need to:

_____

_____

_____

_____

_____

I am able to cope when:

_____

_____

_____

_____

_____

I would like other people to:

_____

_____

_____

_____

_____

What's Finn's spectrum of shutdowns and meltdowns?

Read Finn's poem and consider what similarities or differences you have compared to Finn's profile of shutdowns and meltdowns.

Dear people

Shutdowns and meltdowns
Happen to me
I think they probably happen to everyone else too.
But autism's version means it can be a little more noticeable
That somehow makes them terribly wrong...
Such bad behaviour I have never seen!!
Well I'd like you to know
They're a perfectly normal reaction
To overwhelming events attacking my senses
Or emotions that can't find a way out.
If you had my ears, my skin or my nose
My words that won't speak
These feelings that swamp.
Then I think you would be super quick to join me
In a shutdown or meltdown reaction too.

ACTIVITY H. MY WORKSHEET

What's my spectrum of shutdowns and meltdowns?

Record your poems, thoughts or mini-stories here.

Why don't you write a poem or a story about:

- your shutdowns and/or meltdowns

- the advantages and disadvantages of these experiences

- what you would like other people to know about your spectrum of shutdowns and meltdowns?

_____

_____

_____

_____

_____

_____

_____

_____

_____

_____

_____

_____

ACTIVITY I. MY PROFILE CHART

My shutdown and meltdown profile

Strengths	Challenges
•	•
•	•
•	•
•	•
•	•

Strategies	Goals
•	•
•	•
•	•
•	•
•	•

Top three things you need to know about me

•

•

•

Chapter 7

Know Your Spectrum of Self-Regulation, Routines and Interests

Introduction

Self-regulation

Self-regulation means our ability to manage and maintain a constant balance inside our bodies and minds so we can function properly. With autism, we may be over-stimulated, becoming overwhelmed very easily, or we could be under-stimulated and lose interest in things. Our capacity to self-regulate will be influenced by a range of factors and how well we can deal with all these different issues. These include our sensory sensitivity and processing style, the ability to monitor our executive functioning skills, our emotional awareness and self-control, alongside our capacity to take part in social interactions (POPARD 2013).

Our sensitivity to sensory input, which can be heightened or reduced in autism, will affect how well we can regulate our responses. The protective processing strategies that we use to minimise the impact of sensory issues are our automatic way of self-regulating. Factors like mono-processing or fragmented perception allow our bodies and minds to cope better with sensory overwhelm or tiredness (Bogdashina 2016).

Our executive functioning style may also impact on our ability to effectively self-regulate (POPARD 2013). If we have difficulty switching attention, we can find it hard to change from one activity or thought to another. This means that sometimes we might have problems adjusting our focus and self-regulating our behaviour in order to stop what we are doing. Our minds tend to work by thinking logically in a straight line from beginning to end. We prefer to keep going without any breaks or changes to the pattern of the activity, as it is easier for our minds to keep focused on one task than to change about lots of times. We might struggle to cope with any interruptions to what we expected to be doing and control our reactions. This might lead to a meltdown or shutdown because we find it difficult to adjust to changes, especially when they are sudden and unexpected.

Routines and interests

We need to be prepared for what is going to happen, so we can manage any alterations to our day or routine and retain a good level of self-regulation. Part of our natural way of self-regulation involves developing routines and interests which help to keep our bodies and minds feeling good. They allow us to stay calm, in control and re-energise, so that we find the outside world easier to deal with. We might have lots of rules that need to be followed in a certain way to complete the routine or interest; these can give us a feeling of satisfaction but don't appear to have any real function. These routines and interests are very important to us and, even when they seem pointless to other people, they do have a purpose for us. We like to do the same thing over and over simply because we like it and we don't get bored.

When we are interested in something we become passionate about it. We like to find out or collect everything we can on our special interest, spending as much time as possible pursuing it. We often become experts through developing a very deep knowledge of these topics that are interesting to us, which can be useful in developing a career. It is natural for us to be focused on very specific and narrow topics or activities and often we have less interest in what most people like to do or talk about. Sometimes we can feel down and become a bit depressed for lots of reasons, including our difficulties associated with our autism like making friends or feeling different. We might have a tendency to ruminate and worry over things, which can lead us even further into a negative frame of mind, causing emotional upset (Geller 2005).

We might end up becoming stuck and unable to do anything at all, or have an outburst of aggression (Geller 2005). Our ability to keep a constant state of balance within our bodies and minds will influence how well we can control our emotions (POPARD 2013). We have to be able to recognise and identify our emotions and be able to express them when necessary in order to manage them successfully. We can have trouble in this area, as emotions are abstract and we can't touch or see them, so we might project our feelings onto external things like our interests to make them seem tangible and real. The focus of our interests may indicate our internal emotional state, even if we don't completely understand how we feel, and thus highlight when we need help for things like depression.

These routines and hobbies provide a break from all those things that we find hard to cope with. They can act as a form of protection for us, preventing meltdowns or shutdowns from developing or allowing us to recover after this stage has already happened. In some ways they might help us to process events in our life and allow us to create our own sense of order in a world that can be very difficult for us to navigate.

Self-regulation also influences our social skills as social interactions involve being able to pick up on various signals that indicate what to say or do next to keep the conversation going (Wang 2011). We might not respond to changes in body language or hidden meanings to regulate our behaviour and respond appropriately to other people in ways that would ensure conversations are successful. Experiencing problems with our social skills can mean that we are sometimes left out from our peers' activities, which can make us feel lonely. Difficulties in building friendships and hiding our feelings or autistic behaviours so we can fit in may increase our stress and only make us feel more isolated; while we may appear to be fine on the surface, underneath all these negative emotions will continue to affect us and grow into a bigger problem (Geller 2005). This might result in us having constant feelings of anxiety at trying to hold everything in. Our routines and interests often serve to act as a support system when these kinds of issues affect us.

Being unable to stop following our routines and interests

Sometimes though we can begin to fixate on things so much that we find it hard to change our thoughts and behaviours or to withdraw from our interests. We might have a tendency to do something too much or too little, making it hard to find the balance to keep our bodies and minds at a good level of self-regulation.

We also need to spend time on our own in a way that other people do not need to as it helps us to re-balance our bodies and minds and connect to ourselves. Most people release their stress through socialising, but this often leaves us feeling drained and tired. This time alone is vital to helping us to feel good and we might develop elaborate rituals to complete this decompression process as a legitimate means of self-regulation. While our social imagination to hold conversations can be limited, we might have the ability to develop elaborate fantasy worlds in our minds that we enjoy daydreaming about repeatedly. These can make us feel good and act as an effective stress release, especially if we have felt uptight all day being around other people.

It is helpful for us to be aware of what makes us feel good and keeps us calm, and understand what role our routines and interests play in our lives. At the same time, it might be useful to be able to recognise when we are having problems controlling our routines and interests. This will allow us to enjoy them and make sure they are supporting us in a positive way.

This section outlines Finn's routines and interests and their purpose. It gives an example of a chart for you to follow when working out your own profile of routines and interests.

Finn's routines and interests chart

What are Finn's routines?

- Listening to music repeatedly

- Swimming, cycling

- Sitting in the same chair

What is the point?

- Enjoyment, never gets bored, happiness, feels less alone, time alone, calmness, fantasising, de-stress, processing of events, preparation for social occasions

- Fitness, relaxation, motivation, energy, solitary activities, rejuvenation, positivity, therapeutic, emotional release, sensory release, increases organisational skills, focus on goals and calmness

- Helps her to relax and enjoy her food and TV, can't eat from a different angle now. Her body is comfortable and used to the position of one particular chair, so don't sit in it!

What are Finn's interests?

- Listening to music

- Discovering new music

What is the point?

- Emotional expression, releases joy, happiness and anger, enjoyment, daydreaming, motivation, confidence, positivity boost, comfort, support, identifying with singers and their lyrics, companionship, engagement, focus

- Pure love of music means a never-ending search

- *Movies*

- *Fantasy, release, forgetting things, understanding issues, recognising relationships and common issues, role models to copy, fantasy, escape, solitary journey with characters, identification with stories, companionship, total immersion in another world, no talking needed, sensory quiet time, no limits within another's character*

- *Collecting photos and images*

- *Love of images, photography, colours, nature, movie stars, interesting angles and visual perspectives, make issues in her mind become real and tangible so she can process stuff, express her emotions and thoughts*

Advantages

Keeps her fit and active
Creates conversation topics
Processing and recognition of events
Helps to motivate and achieve goals
Time alone to decompress, de-stress
Lets her mind and body self-regulate
Positive benefits to body and mind
Helps to keep loneliness away

Disadvantages

Individual solitary activities
Distracting from taking part in other things
Becomes obsessed
Can't stop
Would rather be on her own than interact as it interferes with her routines
Can make her feel different

My routines and interests chart

Record your thoughts and experiences here.

What are my routines?   **What is the point?**

_____   _____

_____   _____

_____   _____

_____   _____

What are my interests?   **What is the point?**

_____   _____

_____   _____

_____   _____

_____   _____

Advantages   **Disadvantages**

_____   _____

_____   _____

_____   _____

_____   _____

Finn's spectrum of routines

Event: What was Finn's routine?

- *Walking in circles in her bedroom listening to music for hours and hours.*

Reason: What was the purpose of the routine?

- *Daydreaming repetitively gives her huge enjoyment.*
- *Psychological preparation for events.*
- *Intense release of all sorts of emotions.*
- *Love of music.*
- *Under-sensitive vestibular system means she needs sensory input.*
- *Being alone is essential.*

Advantages: What were the positives of the routine?

- *Daydreaming helps to give a feeling of control over the outside world. She can be anything she wants.*
- *Focuses her mind to visualise goals, which helps her to achieve them.*
- *Energised and positive, calm and de-stressed, nothing else matters any more.*
- *Allows her to self-regulate and deal with emotions with matching music.*
- *Processing of events and thinking things through to work them out.*
- *Better prepared to deal with people and social occasions.*
- *Feeling balanced and at ease. Any problems did not seem as bad.*

- Repetition and familiarity give her comfort.

- Being alone improves her ability to self-regulate.

- Supports her intense need to be alone while helping her overcome loneliness.

Disadvantages: What were the negatives of the routine?

- Spent a long time doing this one activity as she gets stuck and can't stop.

- Didn't want to try anything else. Got annoyed if interrupted or if she had to stop.

- Turned down invites from friends to stay at home to be on her own and follow her routine.

Effect: How did other people react?

- Thought it was weird and pointless and wanted her to stop.

- Ignored her need to self-regulate through movement and music.

- Tried to interrupt as they didn't realise how important it was to her or how she would react.

- Paid no attention as they were used to it.

- Didn't care what she did as she was not harming anyone.

Finn's spectrum of routines

Read Finn's creative writing. Do you think her routines have a positive or negative effect on her life or a mixture?

Finn's routine

Walking in circles
The carpet worn thin.
It seems so pointless
Music on repeat
Limitless daydreams
Makes my world seem complete
As my mind prepares to
speak, speak, speak!

Advantages of the routine

Fading my worries
Bringing me calm
Soothing my body
Everything's under control
It's time to tackle that
awkward social event.

Finn's routine's purpose

Endless hours spent all alone
Never makes me feel like I am on my own.
This quiet time away from the world
Lets me decompress, expand my mind.
As all those sad thoughts disappear.
I'm not different, awkward or socially exhausted
Simply able to be completely free.

Disadvantages of the routine

Was it really a waste of time?
Depends who's judging.
So please don't interfere
Or bother with invites
And definitely do not interrupt!!
This is what I like and
that is the end of it!

Other people's reactions

Tut tut tut!!!
What is the point??
You are really quite bizarre!!!

ACTIVITY B. YOUR WRITING PROMPTS

My spectrum of routines

Use the following vocabulary prompts and questions to complete your worksheet and then write your own poems, thoughts, mini-stories or narrative for each topic below.

Word prompts

Routine and self-regulation: Light, energetic, warm, smiling, alive, buzzing, strong, calm, happy, relaxed, motivated, passionate, habit, obsessed, focused, positive, repetitive, passions, helpful, unusual, strange, regular, unique, dedicated, enthusiastic, keen, constructive, useful, productive, beneficial, inspired, integration, reoccurring, encouragement, stimulated, energised, emotional support, negativity release.

Event: What is my routine?

Is it something you had to do a certain way – eating food, tasks, sequences?

Is it an activity you loved to repeat? A hobby – creative, art, music, numbers, collecting and organising information about your interest?

Reason: What is the purpose of the routine?

Will it help to develop your knowledge or skills in a particular area? Does researching your interest bring you a sense of satisfaction? Does it have multiple purposes?

Advantages: What are the positives of the routine?

How does it make your body and mind feel? Do you get a sense of freedom through focused interests?

Is it a productive way of spending essential time alone? Do the routines provide an outlet for difficult emotions?

Disadvantages: What are the negatives of the routine?

Do you find that you don't want to stop following your routine? Is this a problem or a potential problem in the future? How do you react if you are interrupted?

What feelings do you have in your body and mind when you are following your routine? Do you forget to do other things or neglect them? How do you feel if you cannot access your routine when you want to?

Effect: How did other people react?

Is your routine considered to be unusual by other people? Do they notice that you have a particular routine?

Will they get confused if you are intensely focused on what you are doing and won't change for any reason? Are they dismissive of your need for routines?

My spectrum of routines

Record your thoughts and experiences here.

Event: What is my routine?

_____

_____

_____

_____

Reason: What is the purpose of the routine?

_____

_____

_____

_____

Advantages: What are the positives of the routine?

_____

_____

_____

_____

_____

Disadvantages: What are the negatives of the routine?

_____

_____

_____

_____

_____

Effect: How did other people react?

_____

_____

_____

_____

This section outlines Finn's spectrum of interests. It provides three examples to help you think about your interests, what their purpose might be and to identify one factor that you would like to develop more strategies for. There is also one narrative provided by Finn.

Finn's spectrum of interests (No. 1)

Finn's interest was:

- collecting pictures and arranging displays on her wall. Watching old movies from the Silver Screen era.

Meaning: What might Finn's interest in this topic mean?

- Order and control over the images.
- Immersion in another world that appears to be perfect.
- Simplified version of the world presented through old movies.
- She can see herself through recognising similarities and stories with other people.
- Substitute friendships that she can control, with no negative feedback or need to speak.

Strategies: What else would also help Finn to *feel in control?*

- Knowing that she was autistic and what that meant for her.
- Ability to understand her emotions.
- Opportunity to express her emotions.
- Ability to make friends more easily.
- Being listened to, feeling understood and being accepted.

Finn's spectrum of interests (No. 2)

Finn's interest was:

- intensely reading stories or watching shows about anything to do with negative or sad themes.

Meaning: What might Finn's interest in this topic mean?

- Reading and watching television generally helps her to observe other people's lives to piece feelings together and to understand events.

- A way of expressing her negative emotions.

- How she is feeling is not always expressed the way other people would expect.

- She does not seem or feel depressed, but her interest in negative/sad topics is extreme, which might indicate an underlying issue.

- Fixation on negative themes could suggest underlying depression.

Strategies: What else would also help Finn to understand and express her feelings?

- Journaling – describing specific events and/or relationships and thus beginning to understand what has happened and how she feels.

- Creating a collage of images that shows how she feels inside that she can keep adding to when needed – magazines, internet images, art, personal sketches.

- Creative or physical activities to express her emotions and give a sense of purpose – art and crafts, dance, boxing, running, developing additional more positive interests.

Finn's spectrum of interests (No. 3)

Finn's interest was:

- *writing all the time about everything!*

Meaning: What might Finn's interest mean?

- *Provides a way of expressing herself*

- *To process emotions and understand events or other relationships.*

- *Enables her to release any negative feelings.*

- *A way of getting to know herself better.*

- *Helps her to reflect and see the whole picture.*

- *Allows her to explore and inspire her creativity.*

- *Never gets bored writing and helps her achieve goals and dreams like writing books!*

Strategies: What else would further help Finn to get to know herself better?

- *Take on physical challenges to discover her personal strengths and limits under pressure – run a marathon, trek a mountain, do a triathlon!*

- *Do something that frightens her to find out how much she can overcome!*

- *Identify all her good points and create a **Positive Me** vision board to write statements that celebrate everything that is good about her.*

Finn's spectrum of interests: Writing

Read Finn's narrative for the second example. Do you identify with Finn's interest? Do you feel the same way about writing or something else?

I never knew I could write a poem
Nor dreamt these words would find me
To lead the way
Beyond my mind
Turn empty space
Into this story.

An obsession
Or a passion
It doesn't matter how it's defined

The words appear
Somehow I am changed
Perhaps this is my sanctuary.

Whatever it is
I do not care
Only that I can.

ACTIVITY D. YOUR WRITING PROMPTS

My spectrum of interests

Use the following vocabulary prompts and questions to complete your three worksheets and then write your own poems, thoughts, mini-stories or narrative for each topic below.

Word prompts

Interests: Freedom, comprehension, perception, diversion, control, order, idealisation, idols, heroes, all-consuming, unusual, fanatical, perfectionist, fixated, fervent, dedicated, enthusiastic, keen, withdrawal, protection, interested, emotional support, release, emotionally blocked, confusion, clarity, avid, depression, elation, gratification, satisfaction, happiness, positive detachment from problems, negative detachment from society, safe, isolation, valuable, useful, productive, peaceful, contentment, warmth, passion, dedication, anxiety.

My interest was:

You need no prompts!

Meaning: What might my interest in this topic mean?

Do you think that specific interests might be helping you to develop your understanding of relationships or emotions? Does it help to use stories, films or music to work out your own life events?

Is it easier to live online than in the real world? Why do you enjoy playing console games?

Does your interest help to keep your mind engaged and allow for you to learn? Do you find that you need to use your intelligence and this is a positive way of achieving this? Is reading or learning about facts and figures fun to spend time thinking about?

Strategies: What else would also help me to

_____?

Could you find other like-minded teenagers who share the same interests to help develop friendships?

Would it help you to create an emotions board with images, songs, lyrics, poems, articles and films relating to events/people to record what they mean to you? Would that help to work things out?

How could you deal with issues like anxiety or fear? Could your family do anything to support your interests and any difficulties you may be experiencing?

Do you know how to tell someone when you need help? If not, what would allow you to get help?

My spectrum of interests (No. 1)

Record your thoughts and experiences here.

My interest was:

_____

_____

_____

_____

Meaning: What might my interest in this topic mean?

_____

_____

_____

_____

Strategies: What else would also help me to

_____?

_____

_____

_____

_____

My spectrum of interests (No. 2)

Record your thoughts and experiences here.

My interest was:

_____

_____

_____

_____

Meaning: What might my interest in this topic mean?

_____

_____

_____

_____

Strategies: What else would also help me to

_____?

_____

_____

_____

_____

ACTIVITY G. MY WORKSHEET

My spectrum of interests (No. 3)

Record your thoughts and experiences here.

My interest was:

_____

_____

_____

_____

Meaning: What might my interest in this topic mean?

_____

_____

_____

_____

Strategies: What else would also help me to

_____?

_____

_____

_____

_____

This section outlines Finn's spectrum of not being able to stop following her routines or interests. It will help you identify your own profile of not being able to stop following your routines or interests.

Finn's spectrum of not being able to stop following her routines or interests

Event: What was Finn's routine or interest?

- *Exercise of any kind on a daily basis and total control over her diet.*

Reason: What is the purpose of the activity?

- *Get fit, be thin and toned, develop muscles.*
- *To feel positive and empowered, hyper-focus on goals, visualisation, time alone.*
- *To re-balance, release negative emotions and reduce anxiety, build physical and mental confidence.*
- *Positive integration between her body and mind so she feels good.*

Effect 1: When Finn could not stop following her routine or interest her body and mind began to feel:

- *hyper-focused; thoughts out of control, nothing else matters, she starts to turn down social invitations and goes to the gym instead*
- *a relentless focused intensity that turns into constant preoccupation with feelings of guilt if she eats something bad or she doesn't work out*
- *stressed, with tense muscles; relaxation evaporates, hunger increases, dress size decreases. An internal pressure to be the best grows and grows*

- annoyed and stressed when interrupted or stopped. This is what was planned and this is what she needs to do right now. Options or suggestions are not useful. This is all she wants to do.

Effect 2: How did other people react?

- Delighted and pleased for her sudden interest in getting fit until she would not stop and got sick.

- Offers of advice on the dangers of over-exercise, over-dieting and addiction.

- Warning her to stop over-reacting and do something else instead as it doesn't matter if she has to miss one day of being fit or eats a sweet.

- Wanted to join in and be inspired by her enthusiasm, but they could not keep up with her and had to stop.

Strategies: What would help Finn to stop following her routines or interests when they take over?

- Timing activities to ensure she takes breaks.

- Writing down how she feels before, during and after her routine/interest to monitor how it is affecting her body and mind and identify if she is still in control.

- Discuss her pattern of behaviours with family or friends to make sure she is able to understand what will happen if she does not stop.

- Research other people's stories online to learn about the consequences of overdoing things like exercise, dieting, etc.

- Try alternative relaxation techniques to de-stress – meditation, mindfulness, dancing.

Finn's spectrum of not being able to stop following her routines or interests

Read Finn's creative writing. What do you think could happen if Finn was unable to manage her routines and interests?

Event: What was Finn's routine or interest?

Exercising too much; I can't take a minute to stop and breathe without thinking 'I must keep going, I can't stop now.'

Routine purpose

Fitness and health
Became my priority
Disappearing food
Shrinking clothes size
Perfect body
Reduced anxiety
Boosted confidence
Increased positivity
Complete control.

Finn couldn't stop

Mind control
Focused goals
Relentless pursuit
Preoccupied thoughts
Muscle tension
Pressure grows
Stress explosion
Interruptions are not welcome.
My system of release
Switches to a system of stress.
It seems that I cannot stop!!

Other people's reactions

Pleased at first at my love of being fit. Then it slowly turned to concern about my welfare as I couldn't seem to stop. I never seem to be able to take things easy, even if I reach the point where I might hurt myself, because I simply don't know when to stop.

Finn's strategies

Routines are helpful
But sometimes they get stuck.
Creating new habits
Can be positive and good.

Keeping a check on my intensely focused attention
Will help me to monitor and spot
The time to change.

My spectrum of not being able to stop following my routines or interests

Use the following vocabulary prompts and questions to complete your worksheet and then write your own poems, thoughts, mini-stories or narrative for each topic below.

Word prompts

Routine/interests/self-regulation: Passionate, habit, controlled, consumed, obsessed, focused, repetitive, endless, negative, all-consuming, repeat, impatient, rigid, perfectionist, detailed, peculiar, avid, fanatical, fixated, fervent, unconstructive, negative, stuck, disadvantages, addicted, rhythmic, reoccurring, enthusiastic, keen, excel.

Event: What is my routine or interest?

Did it involve developing a project – art, dance, history, geography, numbers, dates, animals, nature, space, science? Is it a hobby – art, crafts, sports? Does it involve technology – online networking, playing computer games?

Reason: What is the purpose of the activity?

How does this routine/interest help you? What is important about it that you want or need to keep pursuing it?

Does it have a specific function – regulating emotions, releasing stress, online socialising?

Effect 1: When I could not stop following my routine or interest my body and mind began to feel:

Why could you not stop following it? How did it make your body and mind feel inside? What kind of thoughts did you have in your mind when following your routine/interest?

How did it affect other people or things in your life? Would you have a meltdown if you could not follow your routine/interest?

Effect 2: How did other people react?

Did they seem to be bemused and puzzled by your attachment to something they didn't understand? Were they concerned about the amount of time spent on your routine/interest?

Did they want you to do something they considered to be more productive? Did they understand the positive role your interests/routines can have?

Strategies: What would help me to stop following my routines or interests when they take over?

Could you learn to develop several routines to allow some flexibility and prevent one area becoming too much of an obsession?

Are there other activities that would help to distract your mind when your thoughts get stuck? Would setting a goal in some other area allow you to change focus?

My spectrum of not being able to stop following my routines or interests

Record your thoughts and experiences here.

Event: What was my routine or interest?

_____

_____

_____

_____

Reason: What is the purpose of the activity?

_____

_____

_____

_____

Effect 1: When I could not stop following my routine or interest my body and mind began to feel:

_____

_____

_____

_____

Effect 2: How did other people react?

_____

_____

_____

_____

Strategies: What would help me to stop following my routines or interests when they take over?

_____

_____

_____

_____

This section provides a summary of Finn's profile of self-regulation and interests. Read through it and use all the information you have learnt about your spectrum of self-regulation, routines and interests throughout this chapter to create your own version.

What's Finn's spectrum of self—regulation, routines and interests?

Finn's interests can mean:

- *Difficulties with issues like anxiety or loneliness can be positively regulated through following routines and interests.*

- *Other people's stories help her to process who she is and events or relationships in her life.*

- *Obsessions might indicate she is searching for something she needs emotionally.*

- *Differences in how she experiences the world means that routines bring a sense of order and control. They give her some degree of power over her immediate circumstances.*

- *An interest or routine can be a very productive way of spending essential time alone.*

- *Interests may be an indirect form of emotional support that can be used constructively to release negativity or increase positive feelings.*

When Finn's routines/interests are positive:

- *Loneliness can be taken away with the dedication to her passions making her forget anything that makes her sad.*

- *Focused and motivated with intense interest that will help her to learn, develop and grow to become an expert in this area.*

- *Her mind excels concentrating on one topic which suits her way of thinking so she does not have to struggle to cope with thinking about all different types of things.*

- *Interests can help emotions to become real so she can begin to process and understand them.*

- *Repetition and decompression bring comfort, allowing her to avoid shutdowns or meltdowns.*

- *Routines and interests are her natural form of self-regulation that help create order and control, allowing her to prepare for the external world.*

When Finn's routines/interests become negative:

- *Invitations to do something different will be turned down in order to repeat her routine or follow her interest, which will lead to isolation in her separate world.*

- *She has difficulty stopping activities, so she will not automatically stop because she is tired or hurt.*

- *Problems changing her focus of attention can mean she might be unable to control routines or interests so they take over her life.*

- *Lack of awareness of how things affect her could mean she will keep repeating behaviours even when they are having a negative effect.*

- *An interest turns into an obsession that can no longer be controlled and she will need help.*

Finn wants other people to know that:

- *routines are never pointless and give something that she needs*

- *interests can turn into obsessions that take over her life, so she might need help monitoring them*

- *she needs to spend time alone to be able to function properly*

- *it is better to let her finish what she is doing rather than interrupt or make sudden changes.*

What's my spectrum of self—regulation, routines and interests?

Record your thoughts and experiences here.

My interests can mean:

_____

_____

_____

_____

_____

When my routines/interests are positive:

_____

_____

_____

_____

_____

When my routines/interests become negative:

_____

_____

_____

_____

_____

_____

I want other people to know that:

_____

_____

_____

_____

_____

_____

What's Finn's spectrum of self–regulation, routines and interests?

Read Finn's poem and consider what similarities or differences you have compared to Finn's profile of self-regulation, routines and interests.

Routines and interests

Most will never understand
I've got a separate world
Under my command.

Being on my own
Is my social time
Finding ways to be who I am
That's not possible in the world outside.

There is no such thing as loneliness
No failures or embarrassments.
With this 100% dedication
Bringing a familiar peace of mind.

The time to question motives
Might appear with a darkened focus.
Or obsessions that take over
Requiring monitoring and assistance.

Routines and interests
Most will never understand
Except for me and you.

ACTIVITY K. MY WORKSHEET

What's my spectrum of self–regulation, routines and interests?

Record your poems, thoughts or mini-stories here.

Why don't you write a poem or a story about:

- your self-regulation strategies, routines and interests

- what is positive/negative about your self-regulation strategies, routines and interests

- what you would like other people to know about your spectrum of self-regulation, routines and interests?

_____

_____

_____

_____

_____

_____

_____

_____

_____

ACTIVITY L. MY PROFILE CHART

My self–regulation, routines and interests profile

Strengths	Challenges
• • • • •	• • • • •
Strategies	**Goals**
• • • • •	• • • • •

Top three things you need to know about me

•

•

•

Know Your Spectrum...The End

We've been on quite a journey
It's taken up some time.
I hope you have enjoyed it
Found out all you need to know.

With these many things we've learned
We can have a better chance
To live our lives
How we decide.
It's all under our control.

Our spectrum is our own
It's individual to you and me.
With our own personal template
We can discover our strengths within.

Now it's up to you to take it forward
Stand proud in who you are.
It's time to let your differences
Bring all the joy that you deserve.
There's only thing left to do now.
Let your autism shine!

Epilogue

Now we've come to the end of our journey in discovering what autism means and how our spectrum of autism presents within each of us. As we have found out, being autistic means our experience of life can be different to other people – that is why we have a word to describe these differences. All our behaviours are the same as people who aren't autistic, it is just that we tend to experience the world too intensely or less intensely and we have an alternate way of processing information through our bodies and minds. That is where the differences are created that make us autistic.

As a lot of the processes involved are internal, this means they are invisible, making it hard for everyone else to understand us. Although, we often aren't consciously aware of all the things that are going on underneath ourselves. What I mean is that we don't spend our day thinking 'Oh I'm experiencing fragmented processing right now and wait…I'm about three-quarters of the way into a total shutdown, or is it a partial one? Oh no…I've got my rigid thinking cap on and I can't see all the options!' It doesn't work like that. All that happens is that these different reactions and responses lead to confusion, misinterpretations or misunderstandings and missed opportunities to communicate and connect. Over time our responses and reactions may become 'Who we are' in other people's eyes. That is why it is very important to know that we are autistic and it's just as essential that we actually understand what autism means for us. By working through the activities and discovering all the various aspects of autism discussed, the hope is that a lot of stress and difficulties can be avoided and we can learn to take care of ourselves.

At the same time, having to work this stuff out doesn't mean that those who are autistic are a 'problem' and 'other people' have all the answers or ability to do everything we find hard. Not at all! Everyone in this world, no matter who they are, has their own set of characteristics with individual strengths and challenges. The only difference is that with autism we have a much more specific idea of how we function. This helps us to narrow things down, and the word 'autism' puts all these differences into one particular context. Although, as we have found out, there is no one 'autism', rather a mixture of different things that are specific to each person with autism and, as we have learnt, our autism can change over time and circumstances. All we have to do is work out our own spectrum of autism so we can take control of our lives and make it work for us. It's our life and our story to write.

References

Attwood, T. (2008) *The Complete Guide to Asperger's Syndrome*. London: Jessica Kingsley Publishers.

Bogdashina, O. (2016) *Sensory Perceptual Issues in Autism and Asperger Syndrome: Different Sensory Experiences – Different Perceptual Worlds*, Second Edition. London: Jessica Kingsley Publishers.

Delfos, M. (1998) *A Strange World: Autism, Asperger's Syndrome and PDD-NOS*. London: Jessica Kingsley Publishers.

Edelson, S.M. (2017) *The Theory of Mind*. San Diego, CA: Autism Research Institute. Accessed on 01/09/2017 at www.autism.com/understanding_theoryofmind.

Geller, G. (2005) *Emotional Regulation and Autism Spectrum Disorders*. New York: Asperger Center for Education and Training. Accessed on 10/09/2017 at http://aspergercenter.com/articles/Emotional-Regulation-and-Autism-Spectrum.pdf.

Greutman, H. (2017) *What is Interoception? The 8th Sensory System*. Accessed on 07/10/2018 at https://www.growinghandsonkids.com/interoception-8th-sensory-system.html.

National Autistic Society (2016) *Sensory Differences*. London: NAS. Accessed on 30/03/2016 at www.autism.org.uk/about/behaviour/sensory-world.aspx.

POPARD (2013) *Self-Regulation and Emotional Regulation for the Whole Class*. Delta, British Columbia: Provincial Outreach Programme for Autism and Related Disorders. Accessed on 10/09/2017 at www.autismoutreach.ca/tipomonth/self--regulation-and-emotional-regulation-whole-class.

Soraya, L. (2018) *Empathy, Mind Blindness, and Theory of Mind: Do People with Autism Truly Lack Empathy?* Sussex Publishers. Accessed on 30/04/2018 at www.psychologytoday.com/intl/blog/aspergers-diary/200805/empathy-mindblindness-and-theory-mind.

University of Sussex (2017) *Researching Synaesthesia*. Sussex: University of Sussex. Accessed on 01/09/2017 at www.sussex.ac.uk/synaesthesia/faq.

Wang, K. (2011) *What is Self-Regulation?* West Bloomfield, MI: Friendship Circle. Accessed on 10/09/2017 at www.friendshipcircle.org/blog/2011/11/30/what-is-self-regulation.

Further Reading

I am Special: A Workbook to Help Children, Teens and Adults with Autism Spectrum Disorders to Understand Their Diagnosis, Gain Confidence and Thrive
Peter Vermeulen
ISBN 978-1-84905-266-5

The ASD Workbook: Understanding Your Autism Spectrum Disorder
Penny Kershaw
ISBN 978-1-84905-195-8

Autism...What Does it Mean to Me? A Workbook Explaining Self-Awareness and Life Lessons to the Child or Youth with High Functioning Autism or Asperger's
Catherine Faherty
ISBN 978-1-93527-491-9

Asperger Syndrome: An Owner's Manual. What You, Your Parents and Your Teachers Need to Know – An Interactive Guide and Workbook
Ellen Korin
ISBN 978-1-93128-291-8

Poetry writing for teenagers

Poetry in the Making: A Handbook for Writing and Teaching
Ted Hughes
ISBN 978-0-57123-380-9

What is Poetry? The Essential Guide to Reading & Writing Poems
Michael Rosen
ISBN 978-1-84428-763-5

For further information about the book please visit the website:
www.knowyourspectrum.com